EVERYDAY GENIUS:
A Guide to
Peaceful Leadership

WENDY KNIGHT AGARD

BALBOA.PRESS

A DIVISION OF HAY HOUSE

Balboa Press books may be ordered through booksellers or by contacting:

Balboa Press
A Division of Hay House
1663 Liberty Drive
Bloomington, IN 47403
www.balboapress.com
844-682-1282

Print information available on the last page.

ISBN: 978-1-9822-6265-5 (sc)
ISBN: 978-1-9822-6267-9 (hc)
ISBN: 978-1-9822-6266-2 (e)

Library of Congress Control Number: 2021901360

Balboa Press rev. date: 02/04/2021

DEDICATION

For Junior, whose unconditional acceptance of my interest in exploring new pursuits never wavers.

For Mackenzie and Bailey, my greatest teachers.

CONTENTS

CHAPTER 3: ACHIEVE ENDLESS CREATIVITY

CHAPTER 4: KNOW WHAT THE SOUL AND
SPIRIT KNOW: LEAD WITH ALL OF YOU

CHAPTER 5: BEYOND THE BRAIN: ACCESS INFINITE WISDOM

CHAPTER 6: THE TRUE YOU HAS ALL THE ANSWERS

CHAPTER 7: THE SWEET RELIEF OF LETTING GO

CHAPTER 8: FROM COLLABORATION TO CONNECTION

CHAPTER 9: THE POWER IN VULNERABILITY

CHAPTER 10: DIVERSITY, INCLUSION, AND BELONGING FROM THE INSIDE OUT

PREFACE

When I had the idea for this book, my intent was to share my thoughts on leadership. As I wrote, I often found myself thinking, *Who are you to be writing this book? What do you really know? You had better quote others' studies or research to prove that you know what you are talking about. You had better provide sources for every term and idea that you use in this book, otherwise the writing will not be taken seriously.* Then I decided, partially just to make the writing process easier, but also because I realized it was what I really wanted, to just write what I know at my core.

The content of this book and my confidence in it comes from many sources—my educational, clinical, coaching, parenting, intimate, and work relationship experiences. You will notice that many of the ideas presented will be revisited several times throughout the book because they are intertwined. This provides an opportunity to explore these ideas through different lenses. And so I offer these words as a simple expression of what I know to be true.

Peace.

—Wendy

Chapter 1
INSIDE OUT LEADERSHIP

YOUR OUTER WORLD REFLECTS YOUR INNER WORLD

IF YOU GENUINELY WANT TO understand what is going on around you, it's essential to understand what is going on within you. Conventional leadership training highlights the importance of understanding what is going on within those you are leading. A leader's concern for their team needs to include what motivates them, what bothers them, and what prevents them from being their best. But even before you can become sensitive to that, you need to learn to connect with your own motivators, your own blockages, and your own thoughts and feelings related to your goals.

Understanding yourself on this level is only a starting point since this understanding happens purely at the level of our intellect. For true knowing to occur, we must move past an intellectual understanding that happens purely in the brain to a deeper knowing that happens within our entire being.

So, let's begin with some principles about the universal Law of Similars. This natural law manifests in various ways and applications in our experience as human beings, but for our purposes let's focus on its relevance as it relates to understanding ourselves on a deeper level. The Law of Similars is the scientific principle that explains how what is happening in our ambient reflects what is going on within us.

Let's consider a simple example:

You wake up in the morning and your spouse accuses you of doing something they didn't like. You perceive their tone as blaming and accusatory. Moving through that rough start to your day, you get into your car for your morning commute and are rear-ended while waiting at a red light. The other driver blames you for stopping short, even though you thought you had been stationary for some time before they hit you.

You arrive at the office, and you get the sense that your colleagues are suggesting that you are responsible for a critical error on a recent project.

What's the common thread that runs through each of these situations? They are all an example of situations in which you might feel victimized. After the third incident, you might stop to wonder, *Why on earth is everyone attacking me today?* This perception that you've been attacked in some way by the people around you might follow you throughout the day. This pattern can reveal itself in obvious ways, like in this example, or it can be more subtle and chronic; it can also span days, weeks, months, or even years of a person's life.

The point is to see the patterns. A pattern such as this indicates an underlying energy of victimization that is at play within you, whether it is conscious or not. And the last point is key; the feeling does not have to be conscious to play out according to the Law of Similars. In fact, it will more often be completely unconscious. That is the problem. We don't even know these situations are affecting us, because we don't know how to use the signs in our ambient to become more aware of what is going on unconsciously within us.

The insight here is to learn to read those signs. Learn to pay attention to what is going on in your ambient so that when you see a pattern, you can look within and ask yourself: *What, within me, is this pattern reflecting?* Then, you can begin to specifically address the internal issue, and guess what? When you resolve the internal issue, there will be no need for it to be reflected in your ambient. The whole purpose of the reflection in your ambient is to make the unconscious conscious, to help you see that there is an issue that is affecting you. Our ambient acts as a mirror, particularly for the things we don't want to know about ourselves. That is one of the strongest powers of the Law of Similars. It will reveal these patterns even if we try to bury our heads in the sand and ignore them. It will hit us over the head with events, situations, and people that will help us wake up to the unresolved internal issue, whether we like it or not. And it is relentless. It is natural law. It does not grow weary of trying to help you wake up. It does not go find someone else to work on because you're not listening.

So, your task is to wake up and take notice. See what these patterns are in your life, in your work, in your relationships, in your health. Look beyond the purely intellectual approach and lead from the inside out, from a deeper place of knowing.

DO YOU REALLY, TRULY LOVE YOURSELF UNCONDITIONALLY?

HAVE YOU EVER ASKED YOURSELF, in a quiet moment, whether you truly love yourself and whether that love is unconditional? Typically, we are our own worst critics. The human ability to judge ourselves is, sadly, one of our greatest natural skills. This supreme ability to self-judge—if we are honest about it—makes unconditional self-love a goal that few of us have achieved.

If asked about it, self-love is one of those things that people will be quick to say they experience. The intellectual mind says, "Of course I love myself, why wouldn't I?" Through my coaching experience, I have learned that when you dig deeper, it becomes clear that the self-love so many of us feel is fleeting and conditional. We congratulate ourselves on a job well done, a task completed, or a challenge we have overcome. These are the situations that come to mind when we answer yes if asked whether we love ourselves.

Self-love is about more than just being confident. You can be confident in your ability to achieve a goal and still not feel love for yourself. Confidence is a feeling related to what you can *do*. Self-love is a feeling that is not linked to an action, behavior, or accomplishment. But most of us aren't even aware of the constant mind chatter that is going on when we don't complete the task or achieve the goal the way we had planned. This mind chatter is constantly judging and is mostly negative. If you learn to really listen for it, you'll likely hear your inner voice call yourself all sorts of derogatory names when you don't achieve your goals, and that is not unconditional love. If someone you cared about failed to achieve their goal, would you describe your love for that person as unconditional if you berated them about their lack of accomplishment? Of course not! Well, the same principle applies when we do this to ourselves. The fact that the judgment typically happens quietly within our own heads does not make it any less damaging.

We have all heard the expression "you can't truly love another person until you love yourself," but how much time and energy do we spend learning to love ourselves and really trying to get to the point of unconditional self-love? For most of us, it's very little.

And what does all this talk about self-love have to do with leadership? Leading others is about connecting with those you are leading on a personal level. This doesn't mean you need to know everyone you lead personally, because you may be responsible for leading such a large group of people that this isn't realistic. You can, however, connect with them personally. We've all seen successful leaders do that. They have an ability to move people without knowing them. A character trait that makes successful leaders attractive to others is self-love. Someone who is constantly judging and berating themselves, even if they do so internally, is simply not as charismatic and magnetic as someone who is exuding a complete, unconditional love for themselves. A leader's self-love is reflected in the (platonic) love that their team has for them and is another demonstration of the Law of Similars at work.

LIVING INTO HEALTH FIRST

IT IS ASTOUNDING THAT THIS topic still needs to be addressed, not only in a book about leadership but in any book or conversation about life. The idea of putting our health first has become an intellectual but meaningless cliché for most of us who claim to subscribe to the idea. We speak the words that health is important but pay only minimal attention to it. The attention that we do give to it is usually within such a narrow scope that we are fooling ourselves when deciding to prioritize our health.

Going to the gym regularly and eating a nutritionally sound diet address one aspect of our overall health. Health is a multilayered concept that we must learn to make part of our daily lives if we are going to lead ourselves with any real capability and, in turn, lead others with ease. Health and its counterpart of disease happen on several levels: the physical level, the emotional level, the level of soul and the level of spirit. Until we learn to accept our true nature as multilayered beings, we cannot begin to truly improve our health.

Yes, diet and exercise are important, but they really are just the beginning. Not only are they a small portion of what needs to be included in our active attention to health, but they can be heavily influenced by the areas that we're not addressing! We will delve into these levels with more detail in chapter 4: "Know What the Soul and Spirit Know: Lead with All of You."

Unfortunately, most of us still believe the conventional health system's mantra that health is equal to an absence of physical symptoms or diagnosed mental illness. We've all reported to so-called leaders that were considered emotionally healthy by the conventional Western healthcare system, who we know were not anything close to being so. That is because this system is not really a healthcare system; it is a trauma and symptom mitigation system. Until we recognize this fundamental truth and start taking our health into our own hands to move toward an optimal state of physical, emotional, and soul/spiritual well-being, we haven't even begun to create the foundation of health we need for living our own genius, never mind attempting to lead, motivate and inspire others.

Without this core foundation of health, leadership becomes a game of roulette. You will only get results where you yourself have the foundation to support what you are trying to inspire others to achieve. The stronger your foundation of physical, emotional, and soul/spiritual health, the stronger your foundation for peaceful and effective leadership. Self-love, for example, is a key component of sound health.

YOU CARE WHAT OTHERS THINK
MORE THAN YOU REALIZE

IF YOU CONSIDER YOURSELF TO be a leader, you may think you don't care what others think of you. You may reflect on tough decisions you've made and conclude that you didn't allow the judgment of others to affect your decisions. And that may indeed be true. But caring what others think of us is a state that runs very deep—back to our childhoods. We learn early, as soon as we're toddlers, how to shift our behavior to please others. Our caregivers clap or praise us when we do what they want us to do, whether it's participating in potty training or learning to put away a toy.

This positive reinforcement continues as soon as we enter nursery school or kindergarten. It becomes clear very quickly which behaviors will be rewarded and praised and which will not. We might receive a sticker on our drawing, special words of praise, or a privilege bestowed on us to teach us that what we've done is pleasing to our teacher. Our caregivers at home mirror much of the same kind of positive reinforcement as we grow up, earning privileges, praise, and even money for acting in ways that please them.

This is all well and good and seems innocent enough. The problem is that for most of us who have been raised this way, no one ever sat us down as we got older and explained that our self-worth does not come from the praise of, and acceptance by, others. Sure, someone might have mentioned the idea here or there, but it was no doubt immediately contradicted by events indicating that to be accepted by others, you had to act and/or present yourself a certain way.

And so this innocent and even useful tool we use to teach children how to perform gets unwittingly transformed into a false belief that we are only as good as others say we are. Even those of us who would consciously describe ourselves as confident and self-assured are often far more attached to the approval of others than we realize. This is essential to accept about ourselves if we are to lead effectively. We need to gain clarity on when we are truly being influenced by our need for approval and acceptance by our team, our peers, the media—whoever we perceive as "watching."

This need for approval from the outside is housed in our false ego, which we will delve into in chapter 6: "The True You Has All the Answers." This false ego is only a part of you, and as the name implies, it is not the *true* you. Unfortunately, it is typically the only "you" that is developed through all the positive reinforcement you received as a child. Children who do not conform to the methods and get the results their teachers and caregivers expect are rarely taught that their lack of conformity is valuable and a positive character trait when invoked appropriately.

To be clear, I am not suggesting we scrap all the positive reinforcement we use in raising children. It does, however, need to be balanced with a conscious effort that helps children understand that even when they don't conform, they are valuable and loved. They need to understand that certain skills and methods may be required of them in certain settings, but those skills and methods are exactly that—skills and methods. These capabilities and tools do not define them and do not speak to their identity and who they are as human beings, just as their results do not. For example, if children were taught not to identify with grades, there would be a lot less anxiety around academic performance, and there's a likelihood that their performance would even improve. Without this counterbalance to positive reinforcement, we're left with fully grown adults who have totally lost touch with their true selves and don't even know when the subconscious need for others' approval is affecting their leadership style and decision-making.

This need for approval can also come from a trauma that has not been properly processed and released, which I have personally experienced. I was well into adulthood before becoming aware that some of the experiences I had as a child were still greatly influencing how much I cared about what others thought of me.

It's 1969, I'm five years old, and we have moved to a brand-new suburb in Ottawa, Ontario, Canada. The cultural makeup of the neighborhood is very homogeneous with most of the families being white. A black family like ours is definitely an oddity. I make some friends quickly, but there are these recurring situations where I'm either called a racial slur by those so-called friends or the word is used in games such as when the first person to be the searcher in hide-and-seek will be chosen. The method used to choose the first searcher is, "Eeny, meeny, miny, moe, catch a [racial slur] by the toe," even though I am one of the kids in the circle. I protest about this, get in numerous fistfights with boys who have used the slur to address me but overall have a pretty fun time being a kid in the suburbs in the seventies.

Fast forward into my forties. I'm at a point in my life where I've now been through an eighteen-year corporate career including two vice president positions, four years of full-time study to become a doctor of Heilkunst medicine, I've done two years of postgraduate study in anthroposophy, and I've been working with clients full time for several years.

So here I am, being led through a guided visualization, and I discover that the bullying I experienced when I was young is still affecting me and keeping me in a place where I am far too concerned about what others think of me. Imagine, after all that time, training, and life experience, something that was totally unrelated was affecting my ability to be the most effective leader that I could be. Now it might seem like this connection should have been obvious to me as you hear the story summarized this way, but my conclusion about the childhood situation was a common one—while it was an upsetting experience, I thought that I had dealt with it, and it was no longer affecting me.

YOUR PAST AFFECTS YOU
MORE THAN YOU REALIZE

THIS IS NOT A BOOK about becoming attached to a state of victimization based on all the traumas that you've been through. It is essential, though, to understand that unless you have dealt with key events that have affected you, you are not only carrying those events around with you, but the lack of resolution is negatively affecting your ability to be in optimal health on all four levels, which means you will not create the strongest foundation for effective leadership.

In my coaching work I have often heard, "That was in the past; I've dealt with it and it no longer affects me." And yet I've worked with those same clients to help them fully process and release traumatic events that were still deeply influencing their thoughts, beliefs, and actions.

A trauma, in this context, is completely subjective. What one person perceives as a traumatic experience may be perceived by another as a wonderful event. For example, a layoff could be perceived by one person as a terribly difficult event in their career. There could have been a strong feeling of being undervalued and cast aside, and maybe there was ensuing financial stress associated with it. For another person, the layoff may have been absorbed as a relief and an opportunity to pursue something that was of greater interest that they might never have pursued if not for the layoff.

Even when we can look back at an event that felt traumatic and conclude that it was, in the end, a great turn of events, if it was absorbed as a shock or trauma at the time, then there is likely still an imprint of that within your being that you are not aware is still there. That imprint, even if subconscious, could be affecting your perceptions, beliefs, decisions, and actions.

YOUR BELIEFS ARE HOLDING
YOU HOSTAGE

BELIEFS ARE PERHAPS THE MOST difficult thing to change within ourselves. They are so powerful, and we are so much more attached to them than we tend to realize. In the context of religion, it's easy for us to recognize the depth and influence our beliefs have on our lives.

Now transfer that same depth and intensity of belief experienced by a religious devotee to a subconscious belief about someone's deservedness of the job title and position they are in. For example, if a leader holds the subconscious belief that "I'm really not qualified for this leadership position," that belief will permeate every thought, decision, and action in their business and life outside of work. And the worst thing about this scenario is that the belief is subconscious, negatively influencing the individual's ability to lead effectively and certainly their ability to lead from a place of peace. Those around that person are subconsciously picking up on that self-doubt and therefore have less confidence in this leader. Remember the Law of Similars. An energetic exchange is going on whether the participants are conscious of it or not, and everyone is affected. It is important here to emphasize that beliefs in this context are false beliefs. They are judgments, assumptions, and false conclusions that we have drawn and continue to draw for a variety of reasons. The conscious leader, then, must be open to allowing these false beliefs to come out of the shadows and into the conscious mind, so that they can be processed and released.

There are many ways to begin this opening process that allows subconscious beliefs to bubble up into the conscious mind. One simple exercise is to do nothing. To sit quietly, for twenty to thirty minutes each day and do absolutely nothing. No music, no electronics of any kind, can be around you. Sit and just allow whatever thought that comes to move through your mind. To be clear, this exercise is not the same as meditation, because in this case you are allowing the thoughts to move through, not trying to move them aside. This exercise can be done while walking, but the walk should be done without any distracting devices, and should your dog be high maintenance, leave them at home. You want to experience twenty to thirty minutes of totally uninterrupted time in which you are not interacting with anyone or anything.

The insights that come up for people during this basic exercise can be amazing. You may notice themes that recur, such as a theme of anger or frustration, that you didn't realize was at play in your life. When that happens, you know you have some emotions that need to be processed.

You may have some beliefs that developed because of specific experiences in your past that are linked to these emotions. Remember, your past can be fifteen minutes earlier or fifteen years earlier! It doesn't matter how long ago the event happened. Once the conscious mind recognizes that these emotions are there, then methods can be deployed to address them. We will address emotional processing in chapter 9: "The Power in Vulnerability."

With time and practice, exercises like taking a half-hour to do nothing will become easier and easier, as you will start to create a pathway between your subconscious mind and your conscious mind. This way, things that need processing will be more readily available to your conscious mind, even when you aren't investing time in doing nothing. Learn to love the quiet. Learn to love doing nothing. Learn to love your own company when you are quiet and doing nothing. With practice you may come to value the power of this exercise and make it a regular part of your life.

When we take this understanding and apply it to the concept of achieving optimal emotional health, it is an extremely powerful approach to moving along that path. How many bosses have you worked for who you think have engaged in this kind of self-reflection? How much better leaders to you think they would be if they had? How many times, when a business decision was made, did you have the sense that a sound mind was not making that decision? How much stronger of a leader would you be if you resolved even just a few of your subconscious false beliefs?

RELEASE THE NAYSAYERS

THIS IDEA IS CLOSELY LINKED to the previous section. The naysayers are the people around you whose predominant communication is negative or judgmental. Even the media can be considered naysayers at times, constantly talking about the doom and gloom of the economy, for example. When leading ourselves, our response to that negativity needs to be, "What can I do to thrive despite what the media is saying about the economy?" instead of, "Well, I guess there's not much I can do until the economy turns around."

Of course, the naysayers may be more directly in your ambient. They may be your peers, your team members, your board, or your critics—and that latter category may apply to the previous three categories. If you realize that these people are influencing you, then the next step is to distance yourself from them in some way. The distance can be established through action, such as deciding not to continue golfing with a peer who engages in negative talk the entire time you are together.

The release can also happen within your mind. If someone on your team, for example, is constantly focused on the negative, you may create a conscious barrier in your mind to simply not allow that person's words to penetrate you. When you hear the negativity, create an image of a wall that their words bounce off of, rather than take them in. You can even imagine that the words are going in one ear but out the other, as the saying goes. The point is to use a visual tool or a phrase that will help you not to get pulled in by the unhelpful words and actions. You may need to continue working with that person, but you can make the internal decision to release their negativity.

The most difficult part of releasing these naysayers occurs when you realize that one of the naysayers in your ambient is a good friend or colleague. Your initial plan might be to just mentally release that negativity, as described above. But if you spend a lot of time with them, then you'll soon realize this will not be as effective because that person will want to engage you in the negative dialogue. You can't release their negative words if you're saying the words yourself while in conversation with the person. So, the conclusion you'll come to is that you need to spend less time with that individual. Of course, speaking to them about your new focus on positivity is an option, but if it falls on deaf ears, you need to be prepared to release that naysayer. As difficult as that can be, you will be happier, healthier, and a better leader once you execute that decision.

IT DOESN'T HAVE TO BE
LONELY AT THE TOP

THE EXPRESSION "IT'S LONELY AT the top" doesn't only apply to leaders of teams. Simply having the courage to live according to what is true for you is a basic element of true leadership, and walking this path can be a lonely one. Previously enjoyable relationships may fall away as you expand and grow in ways that are not necessarily appealing to those who you connected with before your evolution began. If you don't learn to love your own company, that willingness to live within your own truth will be more difficult because it can take time and effort to develop new relationships that are better aligned with you and your new priorities. In the meantime, you may find yourself spending a lot more time alone, which can be tons of fun if you love your own company.

For many leaders, learning to love their own company is not an easy exercise. Even though you might have spent many long hours working late on your own, your focus in those instances was on completing work, so you may have never learned to simply enjoy your own company. The exercise in doing nothing that I described earlier in this chapter has the double benefit of enhancing your ability to love your own company. Try doing it daily for a few months, and you may find that you start to miss your alone time when you don't get it. The connection between this concept and learning to love yourself is so strong.

Another simple tool for learning to enjoy time with yourself is to pick up a hobby that you've dropped or start a new one that you've been leaving for when you have the proverbial "more time." Giving yourself permission to prioritize activities purely for the sake of enjoyment, without any attachment to achievement, is an essential element of learning to love your own company. So, pick something, even a small thing, that you love and give yourself permission to do it. Even if it's just for twenty minutes. Maybe it's listening to the music you loved when you were growing up. Maybe it's visiting an art gallery. Maybe it's playing tennis with your kid. Schedule one activity you enjoy in your calendar on a weekly basis, no matter how seemingly small that activity is.

DECISION-MAKING IS EASY WHEN YOU KNOW YOUR TRUTH

WHEN YOU START INVESTING MORE time in yourself this way, you'll start to create a deeper connection with the true you. Answers that you may have been searching for will start to bubble up into your conscious mind. Listen to the self-talk that emerges. If you weren't hearing this voice before, it may be surprising to realize how much it has to say. If you were previously aware of it, then you might find that the content starts to shift. You will likely discover an increased sense of clarity around what needs to be addressed. The items that your conscious mind was previously avoiding but that on some level you knew were there, will become clearer. Maybe it's a team member who is not working out. Maybe there is a strategic decision that you've been avoiding that you know must be made a priority. Or perhaps you can see clearly that there is a relationship issue with a team member that isn't overt, but you have always known it was there. Now it's front and center, and you can address it more easily.

Seeing what's not working can be upsetting and daunting at first, but the clarity pays off in the end because you're now able to make decisions that need to be made. These issues are not going to resolve themselves if they are ignored or suppressed. The fascinating thing is that by not deliberately thinking about your work, business, or life, questions and answers that need your attention will surface. Perhaps a creative idea for a new product line or a solution to a challenge that has been affecting your business has moved into you.

This channel that you are creating to the true you makes decision-making so much easier. The human brain is both an asset and liability. Our ability to think about every possible variable and all the possible solutions can be a huge liability and can get in the way of sound decision-making. The intellect is a powerful tool, but we can get into the habit of spinning decisions around in our intellect forever, when our true self already knows the decision we want to make. Once we begin to open the channel to our true selves, access to faster and more effective decision-making is at hand. When you start to make decisions from a place of your personal truth, you will know it. You will make them faster. They will lead to better results. And you will second-guess your decisions much less often.

CONFIDENCE CAN BE AN ILLUSION

CONFIDENCE AND LEADERSHIP GO HAND in hand, right? Or at least that is the common assumption. We think it's logical that a leader must be confident, and many leaders would describe themselves as such. But just like the issue of self-love, a little deeper exploration often uncovers lack of confidence more often than the logical mind would conclude. It's well known that many people who appear to be confident are instead quite insecure, and their bold actions are designed by their false selves to convince their true selves that they are indeed confident.

The key for leaders then, is to look within and ask honestly of yourself, *Where am I not confident?* Ask this question of yourself regularly. No one else has to know, so be honest with yourself. The obvious resistance to this exercise is to conclude, "Hey, I've come this far, so clearly confidence is not an issue. Why would I question my confidence at this point?" The value is that when you discover areas of self-doubt of which you were previously unaware, you have the opportunity to achieve better results by addressing the blind spot(s).

As a result of this self-analysis, you may approach elements of your work differently. You might decide to delegate or outsource a body of work to someone else. Or to approach the topic as part of a team so that you can receive input from others who may be more comfortable and qualified in that area. To admit lack of confidence in a certain area is to allow a feeling of vulnerability to come to the surface, the benefits of which we'll address in chapter 9.

LEAVE SUPERHEROES TO FICTION

BEING IN A LEADERSHIP POSITION means that the multitude and variety of tasks are likely to be high. This huge variety of tasks to be done spawns a "superhero syndrome" in so many leaders. The superhero takes on a wide variety and high volume of projects and responsibilities, extending their reach and influence in an organization.

Taking on the superhero persona works well for new entrepreneurs, for example, when it is not financially practical to delegate or outsource many activities that are not the core competency of the leader. This can also happen in early stages of careers, where this kind of resourcefulness is praised and might even be one of the main reasons for advancement. Recall the positive reinforcement topic that was covered earlier in this chapter. A similar type of reinforcement happens in a career context for all the right reasons but comes back to diminish our leadership effectiveness if we're not careful.

At some point, leaders need to become more strategic and must start to ask whether they are truly adding value by completing the task they are completing. This concept seems so obvious, but we have all experienced the micromanaging so-called leaders ("so-called" because in my view a true leader cannot be a micromanager), who add little value through their participation in activities in which they don't need to be involved. It seems like common sense, but how many leaders truly step back from this type of involvement as their career advances? We'll address this topic further in chapter 7: "The Sweet Relief of Letting Go."

Delegation and outsourcing are essential for the true leader because you cannot possibly prioritize effectively when you are involved in things that others can do as well as or even better than you can.

DIRECT YOUR ENERGY

AVOIDING THE SUPERHERO SYNDROME ISN'T only about ensuring you are adding value for better results, it is also about avoiding burnout. Elite runners, for example, pump their arms and legs in a very directed and purposeful way to use their energy as efficiently as possible. If they were to run the hundred-meter dash with arms and legs flailing out to the side, it's obvious they would use more energy to get to the finish line, and their results would suffer.

So why then do we allow our energy as leaders to be splayed all over in several directions at once? There are so many reasons—from a lack of conscious focus, to an unhealthy need for control, to an inability to trust that others can do the work as well as we can—the false ego needs to show others that we can do it all and that we have so much talent that we are good at everything. There is no reason an effective leader should burn out more often than anyone else. If healthy delegation and prioritization is happening, then the probability of burnout should be minimal.

THE FREEDOM IN DISCIPLINE

OVERWHELM SEEMS TO GO HAND-IN-HAND with leadership territory. The leaders I've worked with typically describe their situation as far busier than they would like. They've come to accept that such feelings come with the territory. That sense of overwhelm or being overworked comes from two main places. The first is our perception of the demands on our time, and the second is often linked to a lack of structure in our calendars.

The first issue is the more important one and the more difficult to change, because our perceptions are linked to everything from our false beliefs, as previously mentioned, to insecurities, to the superhero syndrome and more. There are so many influences on our perceptions that are important to examine, and we will tackle each throughout this book.

The second issue can be addressed more succinctly. Learning to build discipline into how you move through your workday and your projects will, paradoxically, create a greater feeling of freedom. For example, having the discipline to work on your creative projects for a set time each week by building that time into your calendar will result in a feeling of freedom.

This kind of discipline resolves the "I'm too busy" excuse. It also goes a long way to resolving the feeling of being overwhelmed. The discipline of scheduling the work forces us to choose priorities, helps us see when we've wasted time doing unimportant things, and conserves energy as we direct our efforts more effectively. So, get disciplined about scheduling your work, and enjoy the feeling of freedom that results from it.

YOUR GENIUS IS YOUR BIRTHRIGHT. CLAIM IT!

A MYRIAD OF TOOLS CAN HELP leaders define their strengths, but strengths mean nothing unless they are accompanied by another essential element: passion. There are many things that I am good at that I am not passionate about, such as repainting the walls in my home. I am very precise in marking edges and so on, but I would much rather have someone else do it for me.

Not ensuring that passion accompanies our strength is a common error that leaders make. They are told by their bosses, team members, or others that they are very good at something, and so they continue to do that type of work, without questioning whether they are truly passionate about it. They could have ended up in a leadership position because their genius is related to their job but not really reflected in the position requirements. A classic example of this is the technologist who starts their own company with a brilliant invention but has no real interest in leading the company as it grows to a size that requires a different focus.

Each of us has our own personal brand of genius, and our task is to uncover that and claim it as our own. The question then becomes, how do we find this genius that is everyone's birthright? Well, that is what this book is about. Employ the suggestions, be honest with yourself, learn to lead yourself, and your own everyday genius will start to emerge. Leading yourself on a path of claiming this birthright will naturally cause others to want to follow you. Whether you are in a leadership position or just want to lead yourself into the life you want, enjoy the peace you will find as you make this path a priority in your life.

Chapter 2

OVER 80 PERCENT OF EMPLOYEES ARE NOT ENGAGED

CHARACTER TRANSCENDS SKILL

AN INDIVIDUAL'S CHARACTER STRUCTURE IS the foundation for their abilities and personality. Skills can be taught, but if the underlying character structure isn't open and ready to receive the training, it will be a complete waste of time. Skills also need to change as the work and environment change. An individual who has the exact skill set at the time of hiring may not be the right person two years into their employment as the industry and organization adapt as necessary to achieve success. If the underlying character structure is not what it needs to be to learn the new skills required, then hiring for skill set can become a very expensive and ineffective policy.

The character structure speaks to a team member's adaptability, willingness to learn new skills, unlearn approaches that are no longer useful, ethics, intentions in their business relationships, and, ultimately, their performance.

For example, two account executives may both display the useful skill of having an excellent understanding of their competitors in their work. However, one employee's competitiveness might be focused purely on executing the task of selling the product, whereas the other's may include petty competitiveness with colleagues in every work situation, including those on their own team. The latter's competitiveness will, undoubtedly, cause discord and friction within the team, which will lead to lower overall performance by the team. In this example, both employees have a desirable skill, but one has an undesirable character trait that lies behind that skill. The other simply applies the skill to specific situations that require it, without any personal attachment to the "winning" that could be tied to their own self-worth. This is a character structure issue, and this is how character structure issues hurt teams and organizational results.

Character structure speaks to a level of emotional health. It is deeper than the outward personality that a person displays. For example, if we look at our two account executives again, let's imagine that they both have outgoing, gregarious personalities, a skill set that is typically required for an account executive position. They may both genuinely enjoy connecting with others, and that personality trait makes them good at dealing with clients. Consider that while one of them enjoys social interaction and is skilled at it, they don't necessarily need those connections with others to feel worthy or accepted. The other account executive can't stand to be alone, must always be the center of attention, and feels miserable and rejected when not interacting with others. That person has not, as we discussed in chapter 1, learned to love their own company. This is a deeper character trait that will ultimately lead to poor decisions, poor relationships, and once again, less success for the team because this individual will do things to feed their need for attention and outer acceptance, even when it's not the best business decision.

The best way for leaders to easily detect that level of emotional health in another person is to achieve it for themselves so that they can recognize it when they see it. Notice a pattern here? The easiest and most effective way to engage others is to be engaged yourself—not just in your work, but in your emotional health. Be engaged in your life in a holistic way that challenges your own character structure to evolve.

EVERYDAY GENIUS

THE BEST LEADERS SPEND LESS time telling others what to do and more time investing in ways to allow the personal brand of genius in every team member to emerge. Our society's colloquial use of the word *genius* is still associated mainly with intellectual prowess that is measured by an IQ test. Even with all the discussion around emotional intelligence, we still tend to equate the word *genius* with intellectual ability.

I submit that we are all genius in our own way. When we connect with our purpose—that is, the work that we are meant to be doing at any point in our lives—then we are a living, breathing example of genius. It is "everyday" genius because it is accessible to everyone. It's not something that is reserved for a chosen few. Every individual on the planet has the capacity to connect with this genius. It is our birthright, although most people never even come close to exploring their own genius, let alone living it. Uncovering and living our purpose and our genius, simply put, is why we are here. It is the most important element in our personal evolution as beings that walk the earth.

Fostering the emergence of employees' genius is the most important and effective way to engage employees. Since living our purpose is our reason for being here in this lifetime, it stands to reason that the more leaders foster this, the more engaged team members will be in their work. An engaged employee is a high-performing employee—it's common sense.

Employee development programs then, need to focus on helping employees connect with their genius. Skills development is not enough and must be buttressed by personal development on a deeper level. These deeper-level programs will not only help employees connect with their genius, but they will support the evolution of the character structure I mentioned earlier. When someone is connected with their own genius, it follows that the person will be more emotionally healthy. Consider the example of the account executive who needed to compete with everyone. Do you think that person's unhealthy need for petty competitiveness would be diminished when they connect more deeply with their own personal brand of genius and are given the opportunity to live that in their work? Of course, it would! Do you think this would lead to a whole new level of employee engagement and performance? Of course, it would!

ELIMINATE THE WEAKNESS FIXATION

FORGET ABOUT WEAKNESSES. STOP ASKING, "What is your biggest weakness?" in interviews, unless the goal is simply to see how the prospective hire handles a question that nobody likes to answer. What we focus on expands, so why do we spend so much time complaining about what others aren't doing? I'm not suggesting that we completely ignore our own weaknesses as leaders or the weaknesses of employees. But the focus needs to be on strengths and on the goal as opposed to our perceived weakness.

For example, if a team member worries too much about failing, instead of spending time telling them that they worry too much, provide an environment, support, and training that focusses on what the person can do to achieve success and complete mindset work that helps them think into the results they want to achieve. Ensure that the person understands that if they are doing their part, you as the leader will be supportive so that the fear of failure diminishes.

Gallup's 2017 *State of the Global Workplace Report* clearly states that focusing on weaknesses is not constructive. The survey reflects scientific principles that come to the same conclusion. And we also know, from thought leaders ranging from Einstein to Bruce Lipton that we live in a world of quantum physics. Thoughts are energy, and that energy creates substance and results in the material world.

In Bruce Lipton's *Biology of Belief,* he explains how a more thorough understanding of cellular biology led him to understand that the cell has an amazing ability to adapt to the environment. He proves that this adaptability extends to changing the very DNA of the cell. He then goes on to explain that the atom, in the world of quantum physics, is a nonmaterial field of energy that doesn't look anything like the atom with little balls moving around it that most of us learn in physical science in school. This "invisible" field of energy can morph itself to adapt to its environment. If our cells can change their DNA, and we are made up of those very cells, then it stands to reason that we can adapt our thinking and our mindset in the same way, ultimately manifesting different results in the material world.

MOTIVATION COMES FROM WITHIN, NOT FROM OUTSIDE

STOP TRYING TO MOTIVATE EMPLOYEES by guessing what will motivate them. They already know. Just ask them and do that. Really, that is all you need to know about motivating employees and team members. The answers will be simple. Your team members, just like you, are motivated by being able to contribute the best of themselves and by having the opportunity to bring their personal brand of genius to work. When you create the space for that to happen, your team will be wildly productive and highly motivated, no matter what incentives, facilities, and other programs are in place.

This speaks to why character transcends skill. Someone who is motivated by money is, guess what—motivated by money! If that is part of their character structure, then putting an incentive plan in place for them is valuable. Having a monetary incentive plan for someone who is motivated by praise and inclusion may have little benefit. You can see then, how it's important to ask what motivates your team members during the hiring and partnering process. Someone who needs to be able to showcase their creative problem solving will not thrive in an environment with rigid procedures to accomplish tasks.

I recall being in that exact situation in my career. Among other things, I am motivated by being able to apply my creativity in many different forms and believe that to be one of my strengths. I worked for a company that had a very rigid and specific set of predefined steps for the sales process. There was no interest in hearing my ideas about how to accelerate the process and no support or resources offered to support my ideas for achieving different goals. It was like working in a straitjacket for me and was completely unmotivating. I was totally unengaged because I felt like a robot on an assembly line, putting widget A into slot B according the steps, not being able to offer my creativity or my gifts to achieve success.

The easiest way to get good at knowing what motivates others is to invest the time in yourself to know what motivates you. You must know yourself if you want to have any hope of understanding and knowing those on your team.

Gallup's 2017 "State of the Global Workplace Report" states that only 15 percent of employees worldwide are engaged at work. To be clear, the following are Gallup's definitions of their three categories of engagement and the corresponding percentages worldwide:

Engaged (15 percent) employees work with passion and feel a profound connection to their company. They drive innovation and move the organization forward.

Not engaged (67 percent) employees are essentially "checked out." They're sleepwalking through their workday, putting time—but not energy or passion—into their work.

Actively disengaged (18 percent) employees aren't just unhappy at work; they're busy acting out their unhappiness. Every day, these workers undermine what their engaged coworkers accomplish.

If those numbers don't motivate you to think about how engaged your team is, then I don't know what will. It's not difficult to imagine the incredible increase in growth that is possible with even a small percentage increase in this number. It is up to the leaders who dare to lead differently, those who are willing to trust that human beings are capable of incredible things if given the opportunity.

CREATIVITY IS THE SECRET INGREDIENT

THE PROBLEM WITH THE WORD *creativity* is that it conjures up images of a visual artist sitting and painting at an easel, a graceful dancer moving across a stage, or a gifted writer creating their twentieth novel. People who don't feel they are gifted artists of some kind generally conclude that they are not creative. Of course, the arts are all about creativity, but this word could mean so much more to every human being on the planet.

Creativity is how we got here—we were created. It doesn't matter what you believe about how we got here; it was a creative process one way or the other. Everything in our world was, at some point, created. Every action we take, every thought we have was, at some point, created. When we eat to survive, we create nutrition in a form our bodies can use through the process of digestion. You, as a leader, created your business or the work product you delivered as an employee. If everything we do to exist in the world involves creation, and we exist because of creation, then how can any human being walking the planet not be creative in some form?

We need to understand the true meaning of creativity. When we understand that creativity is at the root of everything, we can begin to connect with a power that we all have. If we can create an idea, we can create a thought. If we can create a thought, then we can literally make that thought whatever we want it to be. Since our work product is just an extension of our thoughts and ideas, then it stands to reason that fostering creativity is the secret ingredient to creating (pun intended) engaged employees. A creative employee is an engaged employee. It's the process of creation that allows a team member to feel that they have made a contribution that no one else could make in quite the same way. These are the engaged employees in Gallup's definition.

So if, as a leader, you are not fostering an environment that creates an understanding that everyone has not only the ability but the right to be creative, you won't be tapping into one of our greatest powers as human beings. Creative thinking goes far beyond having a new product idea. Assembly line workers can use creative thinking to make a job that they feel is tedious more interesting in their own minds. That is an extreme example, and ideally if an employee thinks the job is tedious, they should be doing something else, but the example demonstrates that we can create at the very level of thought. Training your team members how to do this is essential if you want to tap into one of their greatest powers: creativity.

GOAL SETTING MUST BE COLLABORATIVE

THIS MAY SEEM LIKE AN obvious statement, but in my experience, this rarely happens. A growth number, a deadline, or another metric is handed down from upon high by the managers or executive team, and the people in the field are left to figure out how they will deliver on such a goal. Sometimes there is a fake process of collaboration, where input is sought from the people responsible for the outcomes, but their input is essentially ignored. This results in the same demotivation that would happen if no collaboration had been sought in the first place.

There needs to be a fundamental mindset shift on the part of leaders to understand that they will not get better results this way. The current thinking is that we must give team members a stretch goal so they will work hard to achieve it. Well, it's true that goals can drive behavior, but it is demotivating and disengaging when team members have been given a goal that makes no sense to them. It needs to feel like their goal to create engagement. When you decide on a stretch goal for yourself, you are deeply motivated to achieve it. When someone imposes a stretch goal on you, you feel unimportant, unheard, and set up for failure. How engaged can an employee possibly feel in that scenario?

Managers will defend these decisions by saying things such as, "We don't have the luxury of determining the goal. We are influenced by market conditions and competition. If our main competitor grew by 10 percent more than us last year, then we have to grow by as much or more this year or risk extinction." Well, I submit that this kind of industry insight should be shared with the people who need to deliver on the goal as part of a collaborative process. If they see and understand those realities, they may decide for themselves to set as high a goal as the executives would have. The huge difference is that they were involved in the goal setting so their engagement will be infinitely higher. If they don't set the goal where management thinks it needs to be, they are not likely to achieve management's goal anyway. If employees do set the goal where management thinks it needs to be, but they don't really believe it is achievable, other problems will result, ranging from high turnover to infighting and actively disengaged employees as described by Gallup. So, in the end, results will not be better. Higher revenue is not necessarily beneficial if profit is reduced by high turnover and disengagement.

Another excuse that managers will use for controlling the goal-setting process is that "Employees are lazy, so we have to give them a stretch goal to force them to work hard." I would say that if managers believe others are inherently lazy, then they themselves are inherently lazy. Remember this concept from chapter 1? We see ourselves reflected in our ambient. So, if you as a leader believe this about your team members, then it's time to ask yourself where in your life you are behaving that way. Address it within yourself, and watch your view of others change.

When your view of others changes, their view of you changes as well. There is a bidirectional energy exchange happening that feeds your ability to lead yourself and others. The goal-setting process can now happen with open and honest collaboration, in which team members don't need to underestimate their goal, and leaders don't need to impose stretch goals. Watch engagement soar as that happens.

FREEDOM CREATES RESPONSIBILITY

THE FALSE CONCLUSION THAT INEFFECTIVE managers draw is that they need to control their team to ensure things get done. But micromanagement leads to dependent, disempowered, and unengaged employees who can't stand on their own to deliver the responsibilities of their role. The concern is that giving employees freedom for things like flexible work hours, working from home, or problem-solving to a reasonable level of authority is risky.

I was once told by the president of a company I worked for that if he let employees work from home, they would all be sitting by their swimming pools all day instead of working. First, that tells us what he would be doing if he worked from home. He obviously didn't have the self-discipline to work from home and assumed no one else did either. Second, an employee may be wildly productive while working outside on their patio beside their pool, provided they have the tools they need to do their work. Third, there is no understanding in that conclusion that we are not all the same. For some, working from home may be difficult and distracting, but others may find the office environment distracting. I once worked in an office with a desk neighbor who was addicted to the office drama, so working from home whenever I could helped me to be much more productive. Having the freedom to make that choice had a direct effect on my productivity and even the quality of my work, because it took a lot of emotional energy to manage my coworker's dramatic outbursts.

Providing this type of freedom may seem risky at first, but if clear goals have been set and results are being tracked, it will become obvious very quickly if a team member is not owning the responsibility that comes along with the freedom. And that is the key; with freedom comes responsibility. Working at home, for example, requires the self-discipline to complete the work without being in view of coworkers and bosses. When you look at it this way, providing freedom is a great gauge to determine whether workers are engaged. If they are, then they will continue to deliver great results. If they aren't, it will become glaringly obvious, because nothing will get done without a superior/coworker micromanaging their every step. Furthermore, the team members who are willing to take full responsibility for their roles are the ones any leader should want on their team. So, give more freedom, not less, and watch engagement expand.

LEADERS THAT EMERGE NATURALLY ARE MORE POWERFUL

A LEADERSHIP ROLE CAN BE FORMALLY assigned through titles and responsibilities, but it can also emerge organically in a work environment. Strong leaders create an environment for this to happen within their team. Imagine a team in which each person was an organic leader in one area at which they excelled. All members would have incredible resources within their own team while feeling fully engaged as one of those resources for others.

A leader who fosters this kind of leadership within the team knows that when everyone feels like a leader in some way, they are all more engaged. I can just feel all the skills and personality testers out there thinking, "But not everyone is a leader." Agreed, but consider that leadership, just like creativity, has a broader meaning than just the colloquial definition. There are the obvious, outgoing, attention-getting leaders, and there are quiet leaders who lead through applying their energy in different ways. Someone may be a thought leader on the team and simply by sharing their insights on the state of the industry, become an invaluable resource and therefore a *leader* on the work team.

When leadership is permitted to happen this way, through a natural interest or skill that a team member has, the engagement of that team member increases because they are bringing that particular genius to work. The team members naturally assume greater ownership of and accountability for these projects. Further, their ability to lead is easy because their team members will recognize their natural talent, knowledge, or passion for the topic. When team leaders foster this, every member will feel free to offer their own bits of genius, and everyone wins as a result.

PROCESS SHOULD PROVIDE STRUCTURE, NOT KILL INITIATIVE

GREAT LEADERS FOCUS ON RESULTS and are comfortable giving their team members the freedom to alter parts of the process when appropriate, to achieve results. Remember the company I referred to as stifling my creativity? In that environment, there was a set of predefined steps for the sales process. These steps were relevant and useful—as a guideline for ensuring movement through the sales cycle, as a point of reference so that internal conversations could be clear as to where in the sales cycle a prospective customer was, for assigning resources, and so on. It is not to say that the process didn't have value. The problem happens, though, when leaders blindly march the team and by extension in this case, their sales prospects, through the steps with no allowance for creativity and other influences throughout the process.

Great leaders know this. They know that rules and processes are wonderful tools, if used within the context of the ever-changing world we live in and within the context of team members having input as to when and whether a particular step of the process doesn't apply in a specific situation. Forcing employees to blindly follow process steps without thinking kills creativity and engagement. A team member who is not thinking creatively or looking for a better, faster, or cheaper way to accomplish a result but says, "Well, they can't fire me; I've followed all the steps," is not an engaged employee but is, sadly, a common occurrence.

POLITICS KILL ENGAGEMENT

WHERE THERE ARE PEOPLE, THERE are politics, because politics come from the false ego's influence in our lives. We'll discuss the false ego more in chapter 6, but it is responsible for all the distractions associated with playing politics in the workplace. As a leader, the key is to do what you can to minimize them. The first step in doing so is to do your own internal work, because when you are firmly rooted in who you are, why you are in the role, and what you are trying to achieve, then the noise of others engaged in politics has less of an effect on you. This then sets the tone for your team.

Will you be influenced by an employee who is constantly trying to get your attention for things that aren't relevant when you are clear within yourself on your priorities? Not likely. Will you lose sleep over a team member having lunch with your CEO when you are clear within yourself on your priorities? Not likely. Will you be inclined to malign another team member to gain favor with your CEO when you are clear within yourself on your priorities? Not likely.

When leaders play politics or allow them to go unchecked within their team, everyone loses sight of priorities, and engagement decreases. How can employees possibly be passionate about their work and actively looking for ways to innovate when they are wasting half their time looking over their shoulder for the ever-present negative consequences of politics affecting their work life? They can't, and they won't, so you as a leader need to eradicate it from your team.

GIVE ACCURATE PRAISE OFTEN

PRAISING TEAM MEMBERS FOR THEIR work seems so obvious that it's not worth mentioning. But when it's one of the questions on Gallup's survey and only 15 percent of the global workplace is considered engaged, then it obviously needs to be addressed. As a starting point, I would ask leaders: "How often do you praise yourself?" Listen to the voice in your head for a while. Invest some time in the "doing nothing" exercise mentioned in chapter 1. How often after a week of doing this, have you heard your inner voice praise you? My bet is that unless you've invested in your inner development, you will go an entire week and not hear a word of self-praise.

You know what comes next: if you're not praising yourself easily and regularly, it can be easy to forget to praise others. Of course, the praise given must be genuine. If it's not, then politics are at play, and it will not motivate the team member at all.

The other element of giving praise and acknowledging a team member's input is to ensure the right acknowledgement is given to the right person in the right context. If a team member has contributed an innovative idea and the boss takes credit for the idea, that is incredibly damaging, yet we know it happens all the time. Taking credit for a team member's work is such a shortsighted thing to do, for the obvious reason that it creates a less engaged team member. But it also shows poor leadership skills to the leader above you. For example, if a VP takes full credit for an innovative idea from a direct report, the CEO will not have a sense that the VP is fostering innovation on their team. If the CEO is a strong leader, they will be looking for that in a VP, so the VP is not only hurting the direct report but is hurting themselves in the eye of the CEO.

DON'T HIRE SMART PEOPLE AND THEN TREAT THEM LIKE IDIOTS

"THEY HIRE SMART PEOPLE, THEN treat us like idiots." Unfortunately, that was a phrase I uttered often to my coworkers in more than one company that I worked for over the years. It is incredibly demotivating to be treated like a fool, and a smart leader knows that the team members are just as smart as their leader. As a leader, it is essential to realize that your leadership position does not necessarily imply superior intelligence over your team members. Leaders who treat their employees like idiots lose credibility and effectiveness as leaders and diminish engagement.

For example, implementing guidelines that are presented in one way when the true intention has obviously not been openly communicated is a ploy that team members will see through immediately. Leaders who do this often sabotage the engagement of their employees, yet I have seen it happen numerous times in the workplace.

An obvious example was an employee satisfaction survey that I completed at one of my employers. The questions were asked in such a way that there was little room to express any of our genuine concerns about the work environment. Instead of the survey being used to improve employee engagement, it was really a tool for the company to use for recruiting, public relations, or some other agenda, to indicate that people loved working there. Completing the survey knowing that we were pawns in this game of chess was incredibly disengaging. We were smart enough to see through the game but were powerless to do anything about it. As a leader, if you make the effort to hire smart people, treat them as such once they are on your team.

TRUST LEADS TO ENGAGEMENT

TRUST IS A POWERFUL ENGAGEMENT tool. When an employee knows that they are trusted, the worker will feel worthy of that trust and will not want to lose it. This idea is related to the concept discussed earlier—that freedom creates responsibility. Leadership comes down to a relationship between you as the leader and those you are leading. It's up to you, the leader, to establish a relationship of trust. That means you need to help your team members feel trusted and respected before they'll trust you, not the other way around.

Trust and control are two sides of the same issue. Trusting another person means that you let go of a certain amount of control. Do you trust yourself? Control freaks and micromanagers typically don't trust themselves, and that is why they can't trust others. Learning to trust yourself to handle whatever comes your way in life is the exercise that you need to embark on if you want to know how to delegate to, trust, and engage others.

Chapter 3
ACHIEVE ENDLESS CREATIVITY

THE FOUNDATION OF YOUR GENIUS

Y OUR INNATE CREATIVITY IS THE foundation of your genius. As mentioned in the previous chapter, the problem with the word *creativity* is that we tend to assume it only applies to people who are in the so-called creative arts—writers, painters, musicians, dancers, and the like. Most of our work in organizations as leaders tends to be left-brained work. And really, in the public school system in Western countries, the left brain is overdeveloped, to the detriment of our creative capacity.

Creativity is so much more than generating a beautiful painting or having an eye for decorating. It is the ability to tap into a place within ourselves to develop an idea or manifest a thought that is new. There are those who contend that no new thoughts are possible since man has existed for so long. Whether you believe that or not, we all can manifest, from nothing that we are conscious of, a new thought, idea, or innovation. We do this in small ways every day, without realizing it.

Consider this scenario: If your significant other or your child was in a physically dangerous situation and you had a short window of opportunity to free them from that situation, do you think you might develop a creative plan to rescue them? The chances are high that you would. Your creative capacity would be activated by a motivation to save your loved one from imminent harm.

For a less dramatic example, consider the way you developed innovative solutions to things like building a fort or creating a new outfit for your doll when you were a child, or even solving a dispute between friends. We used our creative capacity freely as children for all sorts of everyday activities, but slowly, over time, this creative genius became buried under the left-brained focus of Western culture.

When you start to activate your own creative genius, it's contagious. You will invite others to tap into their own creativity as they observe the way you do. They may not even acknowledge this invitation consciously, but they will receive it anyway. Of course, a conscious leadership conversation related to creativity is valuable, but demonstrating it through behavior can be far more powerful.

CREATIVITY IS YOUR BIRTHRIGHT

PEOPLE WHO HAVE DONE PERSONALITY tests and the like will insist that they are not creative because it didn't show up in their results. Well, it may be that they are not meant to be a visual artist, but they do have a right brain, and they are human, so by definition they have tremendous creative capacity! Think of our ability to create life itself when we procreate, or our ability to create new cells to grow, heal, and repair our bodies. There is a tremendous creative process happening through these functions, and we can tap into that in our ability to lead creatively.

The problem is that we have become so results oriented that we forget we are born with this creative capacity, and we mistakenly assume that it does not contribute to anything concrete or valuable. But of course, the exact opposite is true. The creative element brings true meaning to our experiences and brings life to things that would otherwise be flat, dull, or uninspiring. Our creative potential needs to be nurtured and supported because it is the place from which new ideas, new ways of doing things, and new solutions to long-standing issues arise. This is the place from which true innovation and genius derive.

ONLY YOU LIMIT YOUR CREATIVITY

THE ONLY THING LIMITING YOUR creativity at any given time is you. Your false beliefs around your creative capacity and what it means to be creative is what blocks your innate creativity from flowing. We've accepted the false separation of the left and right brain, the narrow definitions of what it means to be creative; we may have slotted ourselves into a category of left-brained or right-brained without realizing it. Most of us come by these false beliefs through the conditioning that has been bestowed upon us by our education system and parenting. The North American public education system creates a false separation between left-brain and right-brain activities. Just because the physical location of certain abilities can be found in different halves of the brain doesn't mean that those two halves can't work in a symbiotic relationship when we learn to be with our whole minds. Instead of compartmentalizing tasks into left and right brain, if we focused on using both sides to absorb much of the content we learn in school, we would develop a more natural connection to our creative capacity as our brains are growing and developing.

For example, a student learning about the Pythagorean theorem in math could learn it in a deeply connected way that involves both sides of the brain. Instead of just memorizing a formula and how to use it, the learning unit could include the history of Pythagoras as a person, drawings or paintings representing some aspect of his life history and an essay or presentation to other students about him. A student learning in this way is not just having a math lesson, a history lesson, an art lesson, or a writing assignment; they are learning the full content and context of Pythagoras, his theorem, how to apply it, and involving their creative capacity to connect with him and his theorem in a holistic way. The Waldorf School is one system of education that uses this approach in its programming, but most Western education systems don't. There is a math lesson, a history lesson, and an art lesson, but rarely are any connections made between the different areas of study.

The task becomes to let go of this false separation that we've been taught and accept the truth that this separation is not necessary or even natural. It is far more natural for all this learning and thinking to be integrated and symbiotic.

It is necessary to get out of your own way; examine your belief system about your creative capacity and challenge it. Accept that you have all the creativity you need and allow it to flow through to your decision-making and leadership style—then watch your results improve dramatically.

Examine this now, for yourself. Have you hampered your creative abilities by dividing your use of the left and right brain? If so, then you can undo it. One belief can be replaced with another. Even better, a false belief can be replaced with the truth. Open up to the truth of who you are—a creative being who has the capacity to create everything from new cells to innovative ideas and unique solutions to the challenges that present themselves to you.

CREATIVITY IS AT THE ROOT
OF LIFE PURPOSE

IF YOU THINK ABOUT IT, creativity is really the reason we're here—the reason we exist. For leaders who try to live a conscious life, isn't the connection with life purpose their biggest motivator, their main reason for getting up in the morning? And what does life purpose really mean? Put simply, it means doing what we're meant to be doing. It means leaving a mark, contributing to humanity in some way that is uniquely you. Well, isn't that a creative process? Of course, it is. The only way your contribution can be uniquely you is that you do something or behave in a way that is yours and yours alone, which means that you created it from a place deep within you. You created that way of being and/or those actions and outcomes that can only be attributed to you and no one else.

Conscious leaders, at some point, are going to ask themselves what their purpose is. Living a conscious life means wanting to move closer and closer to living a purposeful life, one that we know, in the very core of our being, we are supposed to be living. That process of searching for and living our life purpose is a creative one, whether we're in a leadership role or not.

TRANSFORMATION IS A CREATIVE PROCESS

TO TRANSFORM INTO THE LEADER you want to be, you need to be open to this creative process. Trust and know that you are a creative being. Let go of your limited ideas of what it means to be creative. True transformation requires a journey inward, to ask the uncomfortable questions. Asking the uncomfortable questions, such as, "What am I meant to be doing with my life?" is the starting point for transformation from a mediocre leader to a good one and from a good leader to a great one.

Don't expect the answer instantly, neatly communicated to you in a beautiful mission statement that rolls off your tongue and makes you feel like you've finally arrived at where you're meant to be. Expect the process to be bumpy, confusing, and even frustrating at times. You may think you have the answer, only to discover after spending a year pursuing it, that you need to change directions. It is a process of unfolding the self, and while some of it does happen quickly and easily, for most of us it is a circuitous path that often feels like it will never end.

The key is to constantly ask yourself whether the things you are spending time on are meaningful to you. Meaningful in this context does not necessarily mean which activities earn more money, gain praise from others, carry lofty titles, and the like. It means that if you took away all the false ego-based attachments that come with that activity, would you feel passionate and motivated when you are engaged in it? Do you want to do that work or activity when you're obliged to do something else? If it's your work, does it feel like work or fun? Does time seem irrelevant when you're engaged in it? Would you do it for free if you could afford to?

These questions seem obvious, but they are like so many other conversations we have with ourselves and others. We know them intellectually but never go deep enough to answer them from within our true selves. People will say they love their work, and it's what they are supposed to be doing, but it's often the false ego attachments they love more than the work itself—the money, the title, the attention, moving in circles with people who value the same things, and so on.

It can be challenging to discover that it is difficult to make a living doing the work that you find most meaningful. In this situation, try to include that activity in your life as much as possible. Note how elements of what you experience in doing that activity can be included in your leadership style. You may find that the increased ability to be present that you gain from sailing your boat, for example, has a profoundly positive effect on your ability to be present in your role as a leader. You may not know how you could possibly drop everything and earn a living by sailing, but when you create space in your life for something that is meaningful to you, your connection with your true self is strengthened, which will serve you in more ways than you can imagine, both as a leader and as a human being. This process is a creative one—you are asking, listening, and acting, eventually creating something that serves you and everyone you lead.

"NO PROBLEM CAN BE SOLVED FROM THE SAME LEVEL OF CONSCIOUSNESS THAT CREATED IT" ~ ALBERT EINSTEIN

THIS COMMENT BY EINSTEIN IS one of those famous quotes that people repeat but don't live. The evolution of consciousness is a creative process that few people attempt. And yet, the quote is repeated to motivate a team to come up with a creative solution to a problem, as if just saying it will make it so. Evolution of consciousness must be a priority for great leaders because it is the process that enables them to live Einstein's quote and bring creative problem-solving into their work from a place they might never have had access to before.

This may sound like a tall order, but once again, the trick is to break it into baby steps, making each step easily achievable. Take a business problem that you have right now and ask yourself questions about it that you wouldn't normally ask, such as: Who in the organization can contribute to this solution, regardless of their title? If we didn't have financial constraints, how would I solve this problem? If I couldn't possibly look bad to others, what would I do? If I do this, what is the worst possible outcome? Creating an imaginary separation between elements of the problem—getting input from those who aren't necessarily responsible or haven't solved a similar problem before—are the types of activities that lead to creative problem-solving. Playing out the worst possible scenario to a decision has a way of reducing the drama and anxiety about making the wrong decision.

Once you play out this worst-case scenario in your mind, you realize that you'll find a way to handle whatever comes. Then you can think more creatively about solving the problem to achieve the desired outcome. Removing the anxiety from your mind leaves room for the creativity, and the more you practice this, the less bound you are to your current level of consciousness and patterned thinking, giving yourself a greater opportunity for living Einstein's wise words.

INNOVATION AND PROSPERITY
HAPPEN THROUGH CREATIVITY

INNOVATION IS JUST ANOTHER TERM for creativity and we've already established that creativity is essential for successful leadership. Fostering creative problem-solving is one of the most effective ways to create a culture of innovation. Innovation doesn't have to come only from the Research and Development or Special Projects team. Innovation happens best when leaders are not afraid to make mistakes and when they create a culture in which any contributor in the organization is not afraid to make a mistake. These so-called mistakes must be thought of as trials or pilot projects that are incredibly valuable for eliminating possible paths, as part of clarifying the course of action.

Instead of treating innovation as a project or a role, it should be something that happens naturally as a part of a culture of creativity. Innovation doesn't need to be thought of as building a whole new product or service; it could be a small adjustment to an existing offer that increases customer satisfaction or reduces costs. It should be a constant, regular part of your work style as a leader, to be ingrained in the company culture so that it is a part of every individual's work style.

The potential for increased prosperity when this happens is unlimited. Prosperity in this sense can include everything from increased revenue to each individual feeling more prosperous because of the opportunity they have to contribute to the success of the organization. This personal connection to organizational outcomes, as mentioned in chapter 2, is essential for employee engagement. This is everyday genius.

MAKE CREATIVITY A
PRO-ACTIVE ENDEAVOR

A CLASSIC LEADERSHIP SCENARIO HAPPENS WHEN a leader asks their team for a creative solution to a problem, but only after the problem has occurred. So, the message to the team is: "When things are difficult or there is a problem, then I want you to be creative." Well, that message has its benefits, but the creative process should be a part of every team member's daily contribution. As a leader it is essential to foster this so that creativity doesn't seem like "that thing we do when we're in trouble." Otherwise, people will unwittingly connect creativity with "we're in trouble" instead of having it be at the root of all their thinking and actions daily.

UNRESOLVED TRAUMAS
BLOCK CREATIVITY

UNPROCESSED EMOTIONAL TRAUMAS ARE LIKE weights that are carried everywhere with you. Imagine that each trauma adds another ten pounds, which you carry around with you, day after day, and over time, you become so weighed down that you are not operating at anywhere close to your peak level of performance. You may be using sheer will to carry the extra weight, telling yourself you are managing, that you are coping. That's just life; the older you are, the more experience you have, and the more baggage you must carry. It doesn't have to be that way, as you'll discover in chapter 9. Learning how to fully process your emotions means that you don't need to carry baggage from past experiences forward with you.

The problem with traumas and unprocessed emotions is that their effects are not always linear and obvious. For example, a leader who hasn't effectively processed the trauma of a spouse having an affair is not necessarily going to be a leader who doesn't trust their employees. That would be too easy! That trauma, along with other traumas and unprocessed emotions, can create a web of results that stifle creativity in ways that are not obvious. Healthy, strong leaders ensure that they are regularly processing emotions and traumas consciously so that this type of block to their creativity is removed.

WORKAHOLISM: ANOTHER CREATIVE BLOCK

WORKAHOLISM IS ANOTHER DANGEROUS BLOCK to creativity, in addition to all the other negative results it brings. Working constantly creates (pun intended) a singularly focused mind that cannot be open to innovation and creativity. It is too focused on one thing. There is not a healthy balance between focus and no focus, between doing and being, between giving and receiving, and many other important polarities. A healthy balance between polarities needs to be happening, because this push/pull, yin/yang dance creates movement in the mind, and movement in the mind leads to creativity. A stagnant, singularly focused mind is going to lose the elasticity necessary for creativity and innovation.

As leaders, we all know how difficult it can be to meet all our obligations and commitments to others. There can be so much riding on our commitment and engagement that it can become all-consuming if we let it. The problem is that there is a point of diminishing returns—a point at which working more is going to create poorer results.

It is essential to schedule time in your calendar for both time alone and time to play. In the play time, you can be alone or with others. I am deliberately using the word *play* here, instead of recreation or some other suitably *adult* term. It is the idea and feeling of play that needs to be experienced if you want to awaken the creativity of childhood and apply it to your leadership challenges as an adult.

Chapter 4

KNOW WHAT THE SOUL AND SPIRIT KNOW: LEAD WITH ALL OF YOU

THIS IS NOT ABOUT RELIGION

SOMETIMES YOU NEED TO STEP out of your comfort zone to know who you really are. For many people, the concepts of soul and spirit are tied to religious beliefs. For the purposes of our discussion here, there is no religious connection to my discussion of soul and spirit. That is to say that the ideas I am sharing are not defined by any one religion. To me, they are universal ideas that are part of the makeup of every human being on the planet, regardless of which religion they believe in and even if an individual is atheist or agnostic.

To further clarify, when I refer to religion here, I am referring to a specific set of defined beliefs that an individual subscribes to. In my view, spirituality is not necessarily tied to religion; one can be deeply spiritual but not be a part of any religious group. We can connect with the knowledge that there are parts of ourselves that we cannot see under a microscope. We can connect with the idea of something larger than ourselves, something that is present but not visible with the regular eye and we can feel a strong sense of spirituality through that connection.

I invite you to openly explore the ideas in this chapter without trying to put them into boxes of belief that you already hold. And if you do consider yourself religious, I invite you to allow the ideas to move through and just observe how they land within you, regardless of how you were raised or which religious institution you identify with. If it's important to you, you will find a way to reconcile the ideas discussed here with your religious beliefs so that you can benefit from them as a leader.

WE ARE MULTIDIMENSIONAL BEINGS

OUR PHYSICAL BODIES ARE ONLY one part of what makes us whole, complete beings. The connections between mind and body have been proven and accepted through much study and practical application. Biofeedback is an example of a practical application. It is interesting that when mentioning the mind-body connection in most conversations, everyone will nod and accept this connection as true. But it is my observation that while people accept the idea as true, most of us do not actually live within this truth. Once we get into the business of leading our own lives, most of us fail to stay present to the mind-body connection and how it manifests in our lives.

Many systems of thought recognize the existence of influencers beyond the mind and body. The soul and spirit are two additional elements that have incredible power over what manifests in our physical body, in the material world around us and consequently, in our ability to be effective leaders. These elements of our being are affecting us whether we accept their existence or not; becoming connected with them is of huge value so that we can tap into the incredible knowing that exists there.

CONNECT WITH YOUR SOUL
TO BE A GREAT LEADER

CONSIDER THE SOUL AS ANOTHER body that is a part of your whole being and just as significant as your physical body. The soul is the seat of your desires. It is the part of you that is most connected to your life purpose; in other words, what you are meant to be doing in this life on this earth. It is where your deepest desires for meaningful participation in life come from. Your soul knows what is meaningful to you. It knows what you love to do. It knows what activities you would do even if you didn't need to earn a living or if you didn't need to impress anyone.

How can you live a meaningful life if you are completely disconnected from your soul? How can you be a great leader if you haven't made this connection for yourself? The answer to both questions is that you can't. If you are doing work that is not meaningful to you—that you don't genuinely connect with on a deep level—how do you expect to be inspirational to those on your team?

One reason most people don't want to ask themselves what is truly meaningful to them is that they are afraid the answer will not be what they are currently doing. They may have invested thousands of dollars in education and years of work in a career, only to discover that it really means nothing to them. This exploration doesn't have to be so black and white. You may find that there are elements of your career that you are deeply passionate about and other components that feel meaningless or do not feed your soul. You can look for ways to increase the former and decrease the latter without necessarily making one gigantic earth-shattering leap into a new career.

For example, you may be leading a sales organization, and the strategic relationships with customers feed your soul beautifully, but you find the element of delivering on quota causes conflicts of judgment of which you don't want to be a part. Moving to a leadership role in customer service may be a way to maintain the strategic relationships with customers while leaving the revenue delivery piece to someone for whom that is fulfilling. This way, the shift doesn't require a change of industry, four more years of postsecondary education, or other significant changes yet serves everyone involved because now your soul is better aligned with your work. Leading from this place is obviously more fulfilling, and it will also make you a more effective leader.

The key is to find the courage to ask the question of what your soul wants and whether it is being fed in your current leadership role. The other reason people fear this type of exploration is that they are afraid they won't know the answer. They are worried there will be no dramatic moment in which everything they have always been searching for suddenly becomes crystal clear and falls into place in their mind. Or they have been asking and no clear answer has come. This is okay as well and is bound to happen when you are first trying to connect with your soul. The solution is to start acknowledging small desires. Start with making time in your life or work for a few small things you enjoy. By practicing the feeling of feeding your soul, you will start to open the gateway to your soul, so that the more meaningful messages will eventually reach your conscious mind.

If you enjoy sailing, for example, then find a way to participate in it. If buying a boat is totally out of the question, perhaps a weekend sailing trip on a rented boat isn't. Perhaps trying to watch sailing events on a sports broadcast is within reach for you. Remember, you are simply opening the gateway. Even if it's just a tiny opening, it's an opening in the right direction. And even if sailing is your hobby and has nothing to do with your leadership role, it will still serve you in opening that gateway.

Practice this connection to your desires in as many small ways as possible. For example, you may know of two routes to the office. One route may be five minutes faster but is a less enjoyable ride for you. You may decide to take that extra five minutes and take the route that you find more enjoyable. The thing to remember is that *anything* that connects you with your desires in a deeper way contributes to opening the gateway to your soul. So, don't overthink and overanalyze it. Just start doing what you desire, in the smallest of ways.

Once the gateway starts to open, your soul connection will strengthen, and you will become more aware of what is meaningful to you in all areas of your life. Soon you'll find yourself creating situations in more significant areas of your life that are more in line with feeding your soul. When you start to operate from this place, you'll notice that others will naturally be drawn to following you. Leadership becomes as simple as doing what is meaningful to you and having others connect with that energy of inspiration. They will then be motivated to do the same. When you give your soul permission to come alive, you give others permission to do the same.

CONNECT WITH YOUR SPIRIT
TO BE A GREAT LEADER

IN COMMON VERNACULAR, WE TEND to use the terms *soul* and *spirit* interchangeably. And while I agree that they are tightly connected with each other, there are some important distinctions between them. The spirit, as differentiated from the soul, is the part of us that defines our individuality at the deepest level. It is the "I." It is the true self, which is separate and distinct from any other person in existence. The spirit is the place in which we connect with our true selves, separate from the false ego, separate from our roles in life and others' definitions of who we should be. It is essential to understand this if we as leaders are to find our true center; it is the core of who we are that serves as the basis from which we operate in the world and in our roles as leaders.

Most people live their entire lives without having a sense of who they are at the core. They die without having a sense of what it means to connect with their truth, without regard for outer influences. They cannot separate themselves from their roles as child, parent, friend, spouse, sibling, CEO, volunteer, businessperson, writer, athlete, teacher, religious devotee, and so on. They go through their lives moving from role to role, never really connecting with the truth of who they are when they separate themselves from the roles in which they operate.

This inability to separate ourselves from our roles is at the root of so many emotional problems. If someone is highly identified with their role as a successful C-level executive, and they are let go, what happens? The person can suddenly feel like they have nothing and are nothing, because they have not developed a sense of self outside of the role.

This attachment to our roles goes beyond career for most of us, and it starts early on. This is one of the problems with assigning marks to young children in school. They quickly identify with the mark as a reflection of who they are instead of the truth, which is that the mark simply reflects how they performed on a specific assignment on a specific day. The so-called

A student who suddenly has difficulty in a course becomes depressed and the person's self-esteem plummets, because they identified with being an A student until that point in time. When that role no longer fits because the student received a lower mark, they mistakenly question who they are as a person, feeling like a failure and like the ground has shifted beneath them.

When we identify so deeply with roles, the ground shifting beneath us is exactly how it can feel when something related to that role does not go the way we want it to or, to be more accurate, the way our false ego wants it to. The false ego becomes attached to a certain outcome connected to the role, and when that outcome doesn't materialize, we mistakenly connect who we are with the result and use words like *failure* to describe ourselves.

When we connect with our true selves at the core, beyond the roles and false egos, magical things start to happen. The low-level anxiety that plagues even those who don't consciously recognize that they are anxious disappears. The need for approval and acceptance from others disappears. The need for status symbols disappears. The need to self-judge disappears. Insecurities, self-doubt, and petty competitiveness disappear. We become less attached to specific outcomes that have been defined by the false ego, so when those outcomes don't happen, we are not crushed.

The ability to operate from such a clear center creates a magnetism and leadership ability that is second to none. Just like the leader operating within their desire function through a healthy feeding of the soul, the leader operating from their true self at the level of spirit creates an opening for others to be their true selves. And naturally, others want to engage with, learn from, and support that leader.

SOUL AND SPIRIT: EMOTIONAL AND PHYSICAL MANIFESTATIONS

THE SOUL, SPIRIT, BODY, AND mind are all parts of a whole. I mentioned how self-esteem can be diminished when people don't have a strong enough sense of their true selves to disconnect from an outcome their false ego was looking to attain. While the link between a spiritual disturbance and an emotional one may be obvious, it's important to know that the disturbance may manifest physically as well.

We know that someone who is depressed may experience physical body aches connected to their depression. We know that a positive outlook can have a significant effect on a patient's ability to recover from surgery. The placebo effect continues to be demonstrated in clinical studies conducted using the highly regarded double-blind methodology. In fact, the drug effects that are reported in these studies typically include the numbers for those who benefitted purely from the placebo effect. For example, imagine that 60 percent of the group that was given the placebo shows an improvement in symptoms and 70 percent of the group that was given the drug shows an improvement. The efficacy percentage shared with the public in this scenario would typically be 70 percent. When you really think about it though, the efficacy is "10 percent more than placebo." My intent here isn't to analyze the double-blind study, but merely to point out how incredibly powerful the placebo effect is. This would be more obvious to us if we received a more complete description of the outcomes of these studies, and it solidifies the mind-body connection in a way that is grounded in research.

The essential thing to remember is that these connections are real. As a leader, failing to address the soul and spirit issues that you may be having will eventually cause emotional and physical issues that you will be forced to address. Your system is intelligently designed to ensure you get the message one way or the other. Proactively asking yourself the questions that lead to a properly seated soul and spirit will prevent or mitigate a myriad of emotional and physical issues. And, of course, not having to deal with emotional and physical issues provides you with the opportunity to become a healthier, happier, more effective, and inspirational leader.

CONNECTION WITH YOUR SOUL
AND SPIRIT IGNITES CREATIVITY

CREATIVITY OFTEN HAPPENS WHEN WE make connections between ideas or experiences. As you start to understand the links between your spiritual self, your soul, your mind, and your body, you ignite your ability to make these kinds of connections. You wake up parts of yourself that, for most of us, have been asleep for much of our lives. You start to realize how much more there is to you than meets the eye. You start to uncover a whole new world of you, a world full of wisdom and creativity. This is another example of everyday genius.

Since the soul is largely concerned with your desires and your desire function, it's easy to see how your creativity will be stunted if you are not connected with your desires. If you are not investing in learning what you are passionate about and what moves you, how can you create movement in the form of creative problem-solving and innovation in your role as a leader? Imagine the wealth of creative ideas that will effortlessly spill forth when you are deeply engaged in meaningful work that you are passionate about. Creativity at this point becomes a natural part of how you operate in the world.

If you are still living in a state whereby your false ego is dictating your behavior, and you do not have a strong connection with your true self, your ability to be creative will be crushed by the weight of the false ego. The false ego doesn't like change, creates fear and anxiety about failure, and focuses your mind on all the unproductive things that keep you running like a hamster on a wheel. Innovation and creativity are incredibly difficult to achieve when you are in that state of mind. Innovation is all about change, but if your false ego is resisting change, then it will kill the creative impulse that leads to innovation.

The true self, housed in your spirit, is ready and willing to embrace every ounce of your personal brand of genius because it does not create false dilemmas, resist change, or define certain outcomes as failures. They are just outcomes, pure and simple, without judgment. In doing this, the true self supports creativity instead of suppressing it the way the false ego does. Even as I write this paragraph, if I allow my false ego to become concerned about what potential readers will think of it, my creativity and my ability to express what I know is stifled. If I write from my true self, with no attachment to any specific outcome and where I am just sharing what I know, the words emerge on the page in a more free-flowing and less encumbered way.

As leaders then, we must have the courage to connect with our souls and our spirits so that the creativity that is so vital to our roles can be ignited to add value to everything we do.

BEING IN ALIGNMENT
EXUDES INTEGRITY

WHEN THE BODY, MIND, SOUL, and spirit are aligned, you cannot help but exude integrity because you are living in the true definition of integrity. You are honoring who you are by containing the false ego and allowing your true self to come forward into the light; you are honoring your desire function and doing what you are meant to be doing, and these connections create a healthier mind and body.

This alignment will be felt by those whom you are leading and everyone you interact with. You will not have to talk about integrity with your team. It will be so obvious to them that you are living in integrity that they will connect with that, even through their subconscious, and they will know that nothing else is acceptable. They will also want to achieve that same level of integrity within themselves because they will sense how immensely good it feels to be living that way. They will feel your own contentment, your own peace, and say, "I want some of that!" Accepting the leadership of someone you trust is easy and effortless; your team will trust you implicitly when they feel your integrity.

UNRESOLVED POLARITIES CREATE LEADERSHIP DIFFICULTIES

SITUATIONAL CONFLICTS WILL OCCUR NATURALLY in many circumstances. You may be working through the tension between budget constraints and reducing team workload, for example. Consider that many of these so-called conflicts are actually false dilemmas, or polarities, created by the false ego. They are not real problems, although the false ego convinces you that they are. These polarities tend to be fundamental mindset conflicts that we carry around with us regardless of the situation, and though we all have them, most of us have no idea that these polarities are directing our lives.

For example, you may experience, completely unknown to your conscious mind, a polarity of comfortable/uncomfortable. This may cause you to avoid situations in which you are uncomfortable, and yet you may feel stagnant or stuck when you arrange your life so that you don't have to feel uncomfortable. This results in a constant, unresolved tension that leads you to make leadership and personal decisions based on this polarity. Even worse, each of us has many polarities that are playing out in our lives.

A common polarity for leaders can be trust and control. It requires incredible trust to truly delegate to team members, knowing that everything they do reflects on you as their leader. If you have not resolved a trust/control polarity, you will be constantly fluctuating between too much or too little trust and too much or too little control in leading your team. Worse, it may appear to be very inconsistent with no discernible pattern. This creates a lot of anxiety and apprehension as the team members try to determine when to involve you in decisions and when not to. Or even if you tell them not to, they subconsciously pick up on your internal tension and aren't fully comfortable because they sense you don't fully trust them. It's exhausting and counterproductive for everyone involved.

Creating the time and space to connect with your soul and spirit and start a meaningful internal dialogue with them will help to uncover these kinds of polarities that are, without a doubt, negatively affecting your leadership results and your life in general.

SOUL AND SPIRIT KNOW
THE HIGHER PURPOSE

WOULDN'T IT BE GREAT IF we received a clear and succinct letter from our higher selves that explained exactly what we are supposed to be learning in any given moment? Unfortunately, it doesn't tend to work that way. The good news is that we do have techniques for connecting more and more with our higher selves so that we can gain insight on what we need to see.

One simple technique is to ask yourself what is good about a situation that you don't like. Yes, ask what is *good* about a situation that, ostensibly, you don't like. Then, once you've thought of something, write it down. Indulge yourself and make a note of something you don't like about the situation. That should be easy. Then write down a second thing that you like about the situation. Go back and forth like this, about the original issue, until you have basically nothing left to say. What you'll find is that this exercise helps to dissolve a lot of the false ego bias to what you don't like about the situation and displays some insight from your soul and spirit about what is serving a higher purpose in the situation.

Another technique is to ask yourself: *What goal does my higher self have for me in this situation that is more important and even more spiritual than my initial description of the problem?* Imagine that the first answer that comes up for you is to learn more patience. Take a moment to recognize the value of being more patient in all areas of your life, not just the situation that you have in mind. Then, after you have accepted that learning more patience is a worthy goal, ask yourself the question again: *What goal does my higher self have for me in this situation that is higher, more important, and even more spiritual than patience?* Perhaps the next answer is *helping others.* Then, just like you did with the goal of learning more patience, take a moment to really connect with the value and benefit of helping others. Really feel the goal as if it's been fully accomplished. Steep in it and imagine that you really have accomplished the goal and all the great feelings that come with that accomplishment. Then, simply continue this process of asking for the higher goal and feeling it as accomplished in succession, until your higher self simply has no more answers.

You will find, if you practice this regularly, that you will start to connect more and more with the higher purpose behind what is happening in your life—that you, or more accurately, your false ego, doesn't like. Connecting with this and realizing that the problem itself is really a construct of the false ego will help you to resolve problems that are affecting your ability to lead and to live a happy, fulfilled life. Both tools described here will melt away internal conflict and help you connect with your own internal guidance system, which always has healthy answers to serve you, not only in your role as leader, but in every area of your life.

Chapter 5

BEYOND THE BRAIN: ACCESS INFINITE WISDOM

MIND AND BRAIN ARE NOT THE SAME

T HE BRAIN IS PART OF the mind, but the mind includes more than just the brain. This concept can be a difficult one for many of us who have been taught to think about the mind and the brain as synonymous. The mind includes all the intellectual thought that occurs in the brain, but it also includes a deeper sense of knowing and understanding that doesn't come from the intellectual mind. This deeper knowing comes more from the *body-mind;* it is not something born out of logic and linear thinking. It can sometimes be called intuition, but it is deeper than that, and if we define a physical place in the body that it comes from, it would be the torso. There is wisdom in our organs and in our gut, and that wisdom is part of our mind. So, in effect, we have a brain-mind and a body-mind, and we need to engage both to make better decisions and to be stronger leaders.

A neurobiologist named Michael Gershon wrote a book called *The Second Brain,* wherein the title refers to the gut as being a second brain. Dr. Gershon explains how similar the nerve cells in the gut are to those in the brain and that there are more neuro pathways in the gut than in the entire peripheral nervous system. This points scientifically and physically to the existence of incredible wisdom residing in the gut.

Other scientists such as Rudolph Steiner have pointed to similar wisdom residing in our organs. Chinese medicine points to different emotions dwelling, in a sense, in different organs. I'm willing to bet that the term *gall*, as used in the expression "… he had the gall to …" is a reference to unresolved anger that resides in the gall bladder and liver. The gall bladder and liver work very closely physiologically, and they are both linked to anger in Chinese medicine. All of this points to the need to acknowledge that our mind includes this body-mind and our emotions.

Intellectual, brain-mind thinking is where most of us reside because in Western culture we are taught to believe that all valuable mind content comes from our intellect. If only we had been taught that the false ego resides in the intellect as well! Obviously, the intellect is extremely powerful and valuable, but it's far less useful than we think. I say this because we tend to think that *all* knowing comes from the intellect, when in fact more knowing comes from the body-mind. Remember that when I use the term *knowing* here, I'm referring to that deeper knowing that comes from beyond the intellect, not the amassing of information and facts that comprise the intellect, or brain-mind. This is true wisdom.

AWARENESS AND CONSCIOUSNESS
ARE NOT THE SAME

WE OFTEN USE THE TERMS *awareness* and *consciousness* interchangeably. An important distinction is connected to the concepts of brain-mind and body-mind. When we become aware of something, we have engaged our brain-mind only. Consciousness, however, engages the entire mind—both the brain- and body-mind. We want to move from awareness to consciousness because the latter includes the deeper wisdom that we want to draw on as much as possible.

Have you ever been told something is a fact and accepted it as such, only to realize after experiencing that idea that you now connect with it on a deeper level? That's because when you are told something that you simply accept intellectually with the brain-mind, it is just another fact that you know. You are now *aware* of that fact. But if the information moves you on a deeper level or you experience the truth of it, with your body-mind, you are now *conscious* of that fact.

One example that I often see is when I am sharing certain ideas related to my coaching to people who are interested. They may nod and smile and say, "Oh, that's what you do." They now have some information that they relate to something they have already heard about, so at this point only their awareness has been affected. Then, when they engage with me, they experience a shift that is much deeper than can easily be explained through simple words. They are now more conscious, because they have connected with the information with the body-mind as well as the brain-mind.

Things the intellect alone learns can easily be forgotten as new information is collected. Therefore, purely working on skill set improvement as leadership development is limited and doesn't create a true culture shift in organizations. Things learned with the body-mind and the brain-mind together create a new consciousness, an experience that is difficult to forget. You are moved and transformed into something new from this new knowing, and it becomes part of who you are moving forward. No one needs to remind you of it; it is simply part of how you operate in the world.

THE F-WORD (FEELINGS)

WE THINK IT'S ALL ABOUT thoughts because we think so much! If all we do is think, of course we're going to conclude that it's all about thoughts. We live in our brain-minds and identify with our brain-minds, so naturally we think thoughts are the beginning and the end. It is true that thoughts affect us in numerous ways. If we are thinking negative thoughts consistently, we know that we're not likely to feel as well emotionally, perform as well, be as healthy and have as fulfilling relationships as if we were thinking positive thoughts.

Understanding that our thoughts matter is well accepted. But what about the importance of feelings in the mix? How often are feelings and emotions discussed in a leadership and business context? The understanding of how feelings inform and influence thoughts is not discussed as often. But there is a huge gap here if they aren't, because it's the emotion behind the thought that is going to reveal the deeper issues—the root issues that need to be addressed. When we become more aware of our feelings, we will better understand our thoughts. Which mind do you think feelings are more connected with, the brain-mind or the body-mind? Clearly, it's the body-mind. So, there is wisdom in our feelings if we learn how to process them fully. We will discuss emotional processing in more detail in chapter 9.

In the meantime, remember that resistance to feelings impedes the full experience of thoughts, and thoughts lead to solutions. In other words, allowing the full experience of feelings provides greater access to solutions and decisions.

95-99% OF OUR THOUGHTS
ARE SUBCONSCIOUS

MOST NEUROSCIENTISTS AGREE THAT AROUND 95 percent of our thoughts are subconscious. If a whopping 95 percent of our thoughts are subconscious, then why are we spending all our time engaging only the conscious mind? Why aren't we investing in learning how to engage better with our subconscious, so that we can find more ways to access it?

There is some debate as to the differences between subconscious thoughts and unconscious thoughts in the scientific community. For our purposes here, we will use these terms interchangeably; we are referring to thoughts we have of which we are not aware. Dr. Bruce Lipton says that the unconscious mind operates at forty billion bits of data per second, whereas the conscious mind processes at only forty bits per second. So, the subconscious mind is much more powerful than the conscious mind, and it is really running our lives whether we realize it or not. Some will say, "I don't want to know what's going on in my subconscious mind; I have a hard enough time dealing with my conscious thoughts!" Since these subconscious thoughts are running our lives anyway, we might as well know what they are.

Unfortunately, our subconscious thoughts are mostly negative: *You can't do it. Who do you think you are? You're not smart enough. What will people think when you fail? You don't deserve it. There's too much competition*, and so on. Further, when there is a conflict between the subconscious mind and the conscious mind, the subconscious mind always wins. Always.

This is why positive thinking and mindset tools often don't work. The subconscious mind is sabotaging the whole exercise, unbeknownst to the poor student of positive thinking who is working so hard on thinking better thoughts. As Harry Carpenter says, the conscious mind does have will, but the subconscious mind has power. The conscious will is engaged, but the subconscious power is winning, as it is more powerful and works a billion times faster.

The trust and control polarity mentioned in chapter 4 is an example of the kind of challenge that can manifest because of the power of the subconscious mind. Leaders may consciously think that they trust a team member, but subconsciously they don't. That subconscious lack of trust will play out in the external world one way or the other. Leaders will do things that convey a lack of trust even though they've verbalized that they trust the team member, or team members will sense that their leader does not fully trust them, making them anxious and less confident in their decision-making.

If there is any doubt about the power of the subconscious to win over the conscious mind, just look at advertising over the past fifty to sixty years. Advertising consistently appeals to the subconscious mind and the emotions. Most of the messages in advertising are targeted to the subconscious because researchers know this is where all the power is.

This presents a serious problem because it means that we think we're in control when in fact, we're not. Our conscious mind is like the tip of the iceberg, but there is a huge block of ice beneath the surface of the water that is really determining what can get close to that iceberg, how it will move through the water, and so on. Likewise, most of our thoughts, feelings, conflicts, and polarities are playing out in our subconscious minds, and we wonder why achieving anything, including effective leadership, can seem so onerous at times. Even if it doesn't seem onerous to you, imagine the improvements you could experience if even just 1 percent more of your thoughts moved from your subconscious to your conscious mind.

You can take another leadership course based on intellectual learning and keep adding to your skill set, but unless you are learning how to fully process your feelings and access your subconscious to begin to lower the waterline on that iceberg, you're not focusing on the real riches that will create leadership results. Revisiting Einstein's quote: "No problem can be solved from the same level of consciousness that created it," when you lower the line on that iceberg, are you raising your consciousness? You bet!

Creating connection with soul and spirit as well as learning how to effectively process emotions will help to open this gateway to the subconscious. When we fully process our feelings, we become so much more aware of how we really feel and what thoughts are lurking below the surface, influencing our conscious thoughts, decisions, and actions.

With clients, I have used guided experiences to access the subconscious very quickly, but with practice anyone can use simple techniques to learn the basics of healthy emotional processing. We will explore this further in chapter 9: "The Power in Vulnerability."

If the prospect of dealing with emotions is creating some discomfort, remember:

- Decisions and actions are informed by thoughts.
- Most thoughts are subconscious.
- The quickest way to access the subconscious is through our emotions.

As mentioned in chapter 4, we are multilayered beings with activity happening within and around us on many levels. To think we can improve our leadership ability by working on only one level in only one realm is a narrow view. It's like approaching a business opportunity purely from a single factor, such as revenue growth. You might incorporate profitability, operational factors, marketing requirements, competition, and so on into your decisions, to ensure you were including all the relevant factors before deciding on a course of action. Leadership is no different. We must engage all the contributing factors to become peaceful, healthy, and truly effective leaders.

USE BOTH MINDS FOR POWERFUL RESULTS

HAVE YOU EVER MADE A very logical decision to do something, ignoring that feeling or deeper knowing in your gut that was telling you to do something else, only to discover your gut was right all along? Perhaps you made a list of pros and cons about the decision, and the pros far outweighed the cons, despite a nagging feeling that you just shouldn't take that job or buy that house. Later, when things unraveled, and it became clear the decision was not the best choice, you remembered that feeling you had in your gut that you had ignored. As mentioned in chapter 4, you likely ignored it because you've been taught to value the logic and reasoning that happens in your brain-mind above all other types of knowledge.

This is the problem we encounter when the science we are taught is incomplete. We dismiss that deeper wisdom with terms like *women's intuition* and *gut feeling*, relegating this capacity of ours to something unscientific that is only accessible to certain people. Like any other ability, some may access it more easily than others, but it is there, as part of our everyday genius, for everyone to access. The simple act of acknowledging it is there within you will help to open the channel to it.

When making a leadership decision or any other decision, start to ask yourself questions such as: *What feels right? What is my gut telling me?* The idea here is to connect more with your *feeling* than your *thinking*. A simple tool for connecting more fully with the body-mind is to physically place your hand on your belly when you are making the decision. Learning to do this is like anything else. It becomes easier with practice. Practice doing it with small decisions, like which route you want to take to work, or whether you really want to get together with the neighbors this weekend. As you get more comfortable and see the results on decisions with minimal repercussions regardless of what you decide, you gain confidence to listen more fully to your body-mind for more significant decisions.

A classic situation in which this approach can be incredibly powerful is in hiring team members. Someone may fit all the criteria for the ideal candidate *on paper*, and may interview well, but for some reason you sense that the person will not be a good hire. Your gut is probably right. The reason is that you are likely sensing something in their character structure that is not quite right for the position, even though this thing that you are picking up is not identified in any of the screening processes you use. The reverse can also be true; someone who doesn't necessarily seem like the best candidate based on skills and experience can give you a strong impression that they will fit beautifully on your team and be a top performer. This speaks to the idea that character transcends skill, as mentioned in chapter 2.

The challenge here is to ensure that you don't confuse your body-mind with a bias, leading to a hiring approach that doesn't consider diverse candidates equally. This will take some time and practice to discern. Bias happens when the brain creates shortcuts based on perceptions or previous experiences. For example, you may have the bias that people who graduated from a certain postsecondary program are top performers in a certain field. Perhaps some colleagues that you admire graduated from that program, so your brain has created the bias that *everyone* who graduated from that program will be a top performer.

At times, your body-mind may point to a decision that conflicts with your brain-mind. Give yourself some time to muse on the body-mind decision but allow the logic of your practical experience and brain-mind to influence it; you may find that the overall best decision is the one the body-mind points to, but how you implement it is beautifully influenced by your brain-mind, for the best possible decision overall. With practice, you will gain confidence in trusting this interplay between your two minds.

The thing to remember is this: once you get good at connecting with your deeper wisdom, it will always outperform your intellect when it comes to making decisions that are not based solely on data. The reason is that, as I mentioned earlier, the intellect and false ego are wrapped up in each other. The intellect can make up any belief it wants to invent. It can create the most logical reasons to do something, based on a story that serves the false ego.

In this world of artificial intelligence and machine learning, you might be wondering, "But what about using data to make decisions?" Of course, if using data is appropriate for the type of decision you are making, then take advantage of it. But data is often followed blindly when there might be nuances and insights about what the data really means. Data can also be manipulated and presented in a certain way to influence decisions. In these cases, engaging the body-mind can be helpful in conjunction with considering the data.

The true self is connected with the body-mind, your true knowing. It bears repeating that the true self has no need to make up stories based on beliefs, agendas, or ego. It just is. It is just the true you. There is no drama, no need to impress others, no fear of failure or making the wrong decision. There is no fear of having to answer to someone else about why you didn't hire the candidate who looked so good on paper. You know what you know, and you trust your knowing. Imagine the feeling of peace you will have when you connect fully with this part of yourself. In time, you will undoubtedly notice yourself not only making better leadership decisions but being more at peace with the decisions you are making.

BODY REFLECTS MIND

LET'S REVISIT THE MIND/BODY CONNECTION referenced earlier and explore biofeedback in more detail. Biofeedback is a system that allows patients to regulate bodily functions that would otherwise function subconsciously, simply by viewing how their bodies are functioning on a monitor. By becoming aware that their heart rate is elevated, for example, patients have been able to use their minds to bring their heart rate down to healthier levels. It has also been used to reduce stress, lower blood pressure, and even improve muscle tone. Biofeedback is another example of a tool that helps us access what is happening on a subconscious level.

In the absence of a biofeedback scenario, how can we use our body as a pointer to what's happening in our subconscious? Simply by learning to pay attention. We can learn to read the signs. Some people will instinctively say, "Oh yes, whenever I am feeling stressed, I get a tension headache." That is an obvious physiological reaction to emotional factors that most of us already understand.

But we can do more. Chances are that your body is sending a number of signals that you are not accustomed to noticing. If your symptom cannot be definitively connected to a purely physical issue, such as a vitamin deficiency, it may be a reflection of a disturbance at the emotional or soul/ spiritual levels. This is the fundamental purpose of physical symptoms; they alert us to disturbances—even the ones that we cannot see under a microscope or on a blood test. If we learn to use these symptoms for the messengers that they are, we can accelerate our own healing and resolve emotional issues of which we would never otherwise even be aware.

Delving into the scientific principles behind the mind-body connection is beyond the scope of this book, but you only need to make the connection once for yourself to begin tuning in to your body's messages in a whole new way. Not only will this reduce your need for drugs and interventions, but you will improve your ability to resolve subconscious issues that are affecting your physical health, happiness, and leadership effectiveness.

Consider a situation in which you are experiencing an emotion that you judge as negative. As a starting point, ask yourself where in your body you feel the emotion. Once you have identified where it is in your body, ask yourself the following series of questions: What shape is the thing you feel? What color is it? What size is it? Give it a length/width measurement or identify its size by comparing it to a common object, such as a tennis ball. How heavy is it? How old is it? On a scale of 1 to 10, how strong or intense is it, with 10 being the strongest? Write down the answers to these. This thing that you feel may not be an uncomfortable or painful symptom. That's okay, just connecting with where you feel certain emotions in your body will start to open the gateway to that mind-body channel.

When you do have some discomfort or pain, start to ask yourself the question: *What is this pain really about?* Just ask and wait for the insight. If you ask but then send your brain-mind into a fact-finding mission on the internet as part of a frantic need for the answer, you will not likely achieve anything other than frustration. This is a different kind of asking. You are gently asking your body and your subconscious mind to open that channel of communication. Be open to the insights; you can't force them on your time frame and make an intellectual list of possibilities to get a speedy answer. This isn't a brain-mind process, it's a body-mind process.

You might find that journaling helps. For example, if you are exploring your emotions through journaling and making a note of whatever symptoms are flaring up, you may notice a pattern after a few weeks. You may notice, for example, that when you are feeling overwhelmed, your shoulders become tense and sore. Once you make that connection, you can leverage this insight in your decision-making. You can use this physical symptom to more quickly recognize when you are overwhelmed and take steps to reduce that feeling, such as delegating more to your team. Simply acknowledging the feeling of overwhelm may even release some of the tension in your shoulders. This is your own biofeedback of sorts, which you can use anywhere, anytime. Yet another example of the genius within you. The emotional processing that we will delve into in chapter 9 will help with relieving symptoms related to emotional states.

The gut is a particularly powerful messenger of what is going on at nonphysical levels. Of course, it is affected by the food we're taking in, but there is so much more going on here than meets the eye. Recall Michael Gershon's book about the gut being our second brain. Clearly it has something to teach us. When you have digestion issues, for example, a good question to ask your body-mind is: What ideas, challenges, or situations in my life am I not digesting?" You may notice a pattern, such as whenever there is something going on with a certain team member that you have difficulty working with that your gut does not work as effectively. Perhaps it's indigestion or constipation or bloating. The specific symptom is less important than your ability to acknowledge how and when your gut is reflecting some unresolved emotional issues. Imagine the powerful results that these connections can have on your leadership effectiveness if you choose to use them.

Chapter 6

THE TRUE YOU HAS ALL THE ANSWERS

YOU'RE BEING RUN BY
YOUR FALSE EGO

WE HAVE EXPLORED THE BRAIN-MIND, or the intellect, and its entanglement with the false ego, or false self. Recall that it is the part of us that operates based on wanting to appear a certain way to others. It is insecure, anxious, and wants approval and acceptance. Its goal is to protect us from anything new or uncomfortable; it does not like change. For most of us it is completely running our lives without us even knowing it. We think we are our false ego. We mistake it for our true selves. We refer to "I" as if we are talking about our true selves, but we're almost always referring to our false selves—our false egos.

The problem with allowing the false ego to run our lives is that it does not allow the true self to come forward. It is bent on keeping us stuck in negative emotional states, creating scenarios in our intellectual minds that serve it and feed it. So, the false ego feeds on itself and creates scenarios to ensure its existence. It is, in effect, keeping the true you captive.

The false self is never satisfied and never finds peace. It is never content. It does not live in the present moment, preferring to deal with the past or the future in one way or another. Think of the classic case of leaders who move up in their careers ostensibly because of talent, but the other reason is that they are never content with where they are. When they reach a peak, their satisfaction is short-lived because they have no connection with their true selves and must find the next peak.

THE TRUE SELF: THE PEACE WITHIN

THE TRUE SELF, ON THE other hand, is where all the noise and confusion of life and leadership fall away. The true self is just that: you. No one else, nothing else. It always knows what it wants in every single situation. It is crystal clear on what your life purpose is, what you are passionate about, and what is important to you. It has all the answers you need.

The true self navigates life according to its own compass. It is not pushed and pulled by others like the false ego/false self is. Imagine the confidence and power you exude when you are aligned with who you are at the very core. Imagine the ease with which you make decisions and execute them. Imagine the magnetism that you generate when you are living and acting in alignment with your true self. Others will easily connect with this ease, confidence, and power and will want to be in your presence. They will naturally follow because their true selves are naturally attracted to others who are living in their truth. It's automatic, it's easy, and it's natural.

SCHOOL AND PARENTING STRUCTURES BURY THE TRUE SELF

IF WE ALL HAVE THIS true self, then what happened to it? Why don't we know about it and why aren't we connected with it? The Western school system and our parenting styles are the main culprits. Add in the influence of cultural and societal influences, and it is easy to see how we have arrived at this place.

How many of us as children were truly and consistently supported in expressing all emotions? Very few, without a doubt. We are given the message early on that expressing anger, for example, is not acceptable. The thinking behind this seems reasonable. Our parents wanted us to get along with others in group settings, reach certain milestones, and respect others. There is nothing wrong with any of those goals. The problem is that in being taught those skills, we were not taught how to fully process our emotions in a healthy way. We got the message that certain emotions were "bad" or not acceptable to have in some way, or that they were to be kept to oneself—to be suppressed. This emotional suppression is where it all starts. The true self may be angry, but by the time we are three or four, we're receiving strong messages that our caregivers do not want to see or deal with our anger. We learn to "behave" and suppress it. And so begins the suppression of our true selves.

Then it is further engrained in the Western school system. Kids who don't fit into a predetermined learning style are quickly labeled hyperactive or having attention-deficit and a long list of other labels that get assigned to those whose self-expression does not fit the predetermined mold. It happens through positive reinforcement at school too; we are rewarded with stickers and privileges for certain behavior, and like Pavlov's dog, we are trained to be a certain way.

Again, it is important to teach kids how to behave in groups and how to cooperate and interact with others in a respectful way. The problem is that in doing this we are missing a huge part of their healthy development—how to meet all those requirements for healthy interaction with others *and still* stay connected to their true selves. We completely ignore this element of healthy living. We ignore the genius that is the true self and focus on a narrow definition of intellectual genius in the school setting.

Cultural influences have the same effect. We raise our kids according to our beliefs and culture without creating space for the individual—the true self—to emerge within that belief or cultural system.

This pattern extends to our interests. Suddenly, it's only acceptable to our caregivers and educators to pursue certain activities or certain career paths. If you parents worked hard to provide the opportunity for postsecondary education, it may not be acceptable for you to forego that opportunity. Your true self may know that it is not the right path for you at a given point in time, but the false self is in control, taking over your intellect, and you cannot see any other path than taking a course that is acceptable to your caregivers, educators, friends, neighbors, church, and so on. And the conflict between the true self and false self becomes deeper and deeper.

OUR DEVELOPMENT IS STUNTED

As WE SUCCUMB MORE AND more to these pressures, our healthy emotional and spiritual development is stunted. The healthy unfolding of the true self never happens. It is there when we are babies, crying when hungry, wet, or uncomfortable. It is there when we are toddlers, learning that there is indeed an *I* that is separate from our caregivers. And then the suppression starts; there is a reason this stage of development is often referred to as *the terrible twos*. Adults apply this label to this stage because of the inconvenience the expression of individuality produces at this young age. This expression of individuality is not yet elegant, polite, quiet, or convenient.

We see this individuation naturally happen again during the teenage years, often in unhealthy and extreme ways. Again, as adults we should be supporting healthy individuation instead of suppressing it all simply because there are typically some poor choices made by teenagers, who are navigating a new version of themselves. If all of this happens as it should, the true self should be unfolding beautifully around the age of twenty-one.

The reality, though, is that this blossoming rarely happens. What we are seeing is a false version of the individual, who may be independent and productive but who has been so heavily influenced and suppressed as they matured that we are seeing an outer personality that has little in common with the true self beneath the surface. Then the pressures of being self-sufficient create more seemingly appropriate compromises that we justify with the false self/intellect. We say things to ourselves such as, "Well, this wouldn't be my first choice for a career, but there are more jobs available in this field right now." This is a practical and sometimes necessary choice. To support the true self, though, the decision needs to be made within a conscious context of it being a short-term solution, or we need to find other ways to be in our true selves outside of that career choice. Otherwise, practical compromises like these become a way of being that never allows the true self to emerge.

RESOLVING THE CONFLICT BETWEEN THE TWO SELVES

TRUE LEADERS NEED TO HAVE a strong relationship with their true selves. From this relationship with themselves, relationships with others and the ability to lead are accomplished easily. Without it, you won't have the strong foundation you need to lead successfully. Now some of you reading are saying, "But I've already come this far doing things the way I've done them without employing any of these ideas. Why change now when how I've been operating has worked for me?" Well, that's like saying that we rode our bikes as kids without helmets and survived, so why bother wearing one now? The reality is that the helmet can reduce your chances of serious injury. Doing things the way we've always done them without actively engaging in ways to improve does not demonstrate leadership. Leadership means continual improvement and personal development.

Like many other improvements, you won't know how much better it can be until you implement the change. I've seen this happen often with coaching clients. They will insist certain areas in their lives are fine until we delve into them and resolve some issues. Then they wonder how it is that they thought things were fine before the resolution. This disconnect is common and permeates so many areas of our lives that we simply don't know who we are any more or realize that our false selves are in charge.

If you try to lead from the false ego or the false self, you will forever by swayed by the latest anxieties, fears, and insecurities that define the false self. Even when you achieve a goal, you won't be able to enjoy the success because your false self will be criticizing, judging, and restless to achieve the next goal. There will be no peace.

RESISTANCE IS A GIFT

EXPECT RESISTANCE AS YOU OPEN up to these ideas. Just as you need to create resistance to build the muscles in your body, your true self needs some resistance to develop. You could even say that is one of the roles of the false self—to provide some healthy resistance to the true self so that it can develop over time. Use the resistance like you would use the weights in a gym. Be aware of it, even allow it to create some discomfort, but be conscious of it and use it to develop and to give you clues as to what might be happening in your subconscious mind.

How often have you heard people talk about all the reasons they can't start their dream project, so they talk about it for years and never start it? That's resistance, and there is usually something about that dream project that will open something new for them in a big way. The false self does not like change, remember. So, it will create resistance—barriers, excuses, and all sorts of logical and practical reasons—to prevent them from starting that dream project.

Once you can see it for what it is, you can use the resistance as a gift and a clue that you are on to something—that this thing you are resisting is likely especially important to your true self. We naturally resist things that we don't want, such as poverty, but the false self will also resist things that the true self wants and needs.

HOW TO RECOGNIZE THE FALSE EGO

THE IMPORTANT THING TO REMEMBER is that while this false ego or false self may always be with us to a certain extent, we can minimize its effect. The first step is to recognize it when it presents itself. It will show up in different ways for different people and even in different situations for an individual, but the following are some ways to recognize its presence:

1. You find yourself wondering or imagining what others will think of you. In leadership positions there will always be others who are evaluating your performance whether they are clients, team members, or investors. Working toward your intended outcomes is obviously important but being concerned with what others will think of you personally is quite different. The former is simply an intellectual exercise of working toward an outcome, knowing that even if you don't achieve it, others' opinions of you will not affect your own opinion of yourself. The latter ties your own evaluation of what you think of yourself to others' approval.

2. You are bothered or easily offended by others' comments about or actions toward you. This is not to say that you should accept disrespectful, abusive, or unkind behavior. The intent is to distinguish between others' behavior and your false ego's reactions to it. If you are pulled into the drama without the ability to observe yourself and your reactions with insight, your false ego is at play.

3. You are comparing yourself to others in any way: income, title, looks, fitness, education, relationship status, and so on. Being motivated or inspired by others and learning from others' achievements can be helpful, but not when your inner dialogue turns to a comparison that judges you as somehow *lesser than*, because you have not yet achieved those things you admire in someone else.

4. You've said, either verbally or to yourself, that you will feel successful when you reach a certain point that you have defined

for yourself. The key is to have goals without attaching your self-approval to their achievement. You must approve of yourself and love yourself *no matter what*. This flies in the face of how we were raised, as mentioned earlier; we have been taught to attach our self-acceptance to an external achievement of goals, because that is how we received acceptance from our influencers.

5. You feel that you have nothing to learn from others—that you have all the answers. This type of thinking is often referred to as a fixed mindset, as opposed to a growth mindset. In our language, this egocentricity refers to the false ego: *it's all about me, I know best—that's why I'm in charge*, and so on.

6. You are judging yourself and often feeling emotions like guilt and shame. Of course, we've all felt these emotions, and as mentioned earlier, it is important to fully process them. Just recognize that these feelings of self-judgment are coming from the false ego.

7. You are constantly judging others. This item is related to the previous one; all judgment comes from the false ego. To be clear, I am not referring to evaluating someone's performance against a clear set of previously agreed-upon criteria. I am referring to personally judging, criticizing, or blaming individuals. Just sit with those two different scenarios for a moment and ask yourself how each of them feels. Objective evaluations of performance don't carry with them any emotional attachment or negative feelings, even when the performance has fallen short of the goal. But when we blame or criticize others, there are all sorts of negative emotions we feel as we are doing it. That's how you can differentiate the two.

8. You resist change, particularly when it involves personal growth. The false ego hates change, and it particularly dislikes expansion. It likes to keep you the way you've always been, where every action and reaction is predictable and known and, in its twisted thinking, safe. It feels safe even when the behaviors you're engaged in are self-destructive. It is the devil it knows, so to speak. Your false ego will create the exact narrative that it knows will limit your growth and keep you contracted. It will say things like: "Why should I change when I've gotten this far doing things this way?" "That is risky," "Stick to what you know," "You don't have enough time/money/

energy/training for that." and the like. Its voice will sound very logical, and therefore it will trip you up. Therefore, we must learn to hear the false ego as separate from the voice of our true selves.

9. You negate the importance of the body-mind. The brain-mind, run by the false ego, will spin that very logical list of reasons to take a course of action. This is a classic modus operandi of many leaders. Once again, we are not taught to include our whole mind in our decisions, so we are making decisions purely with the part of our mind that is most susceptible to illusion and deception and is least connected to our true selves.

10. You don't meet your commitments, even the ones you make only to yourself. In fact, those are the most important ones to keep, to develop the muscle of keeping commitments. The false ego will make excuses as to why you didn't complete your exercise plan or why you don't have time to pursue that hobby that has been on the back burner for ten years even when you have promised yourself each January that this year will be the year you find a way to pursue it.

This is by no means an exhaustive list. The false ego will show itself in ways that can range from subtle to ostentatious, and it will morph itself into different forms as you grow, to prevent further personal development and expansion. You, the true you, must be vigilant in having the honest conversation with yourself to ask whether the false ego is at play when making decisions if you want to achieve leadership that is both successful and peaceful.

NEUTRALIZE THE FALSE EGO

NOW THAT WE'VE EXAMINED SOME ways to recognize when the false ego is at play, we can explore how to minimize it. The first point to remember is not to let the false ego judge the false ego! In other words, don't be hard on yourself when you reflect on a situation and recognize you were acting from the position of your false ego. Learning to become self-aware can be overwhelming if not approached with the right attitude and with the right care. This is one reason that so many people just don't bother. Instead of using the self-awareness as a tool for growth, they fall into the trap of even more self-judgment and feel that positive change is not achievable.

When you see that your false ego created an action, reaction, or thought that didn't serve you, simply acknowledge it and set about making an adjustment. You may even practice gratitude for your false ego's involvement, if only as a tool to help you grow into the leader you want to be. The adjustment may be to revisit the situation and do something different. If the specific situation can't be revisited, then it may be to ask yourself how you will act in the next similar situation that arises, from the place of your true self.

Once you become clear on that, it will be more accessible to you for future situations. The key is to start recognizing it with a sense of amused detachment. "Oh, there is that darned false ego again, but I see it. Next time I will..." It is like what happens when you are considering buying a new car. If you become interested in a certain model, you start to notice it everywhere you go, whereas before you were in the market for one it never registered in your conscious mind. The more you practice seeing your false ego, the more you will recognize it.

The more you recognize it, the more you can neutralize its control over you. As you do that, watch your true self start to emerge. Watch the reaction of those you are leading and influencing. Watch your results improve because you are aligned within yourself as opposed to that split between your false and true selves that had been at play to a greater extent in the past.

QUESTION YOUR THOUGHTS TO MAKE SOUND DECISIONS

LET'S REVISIT THE TOPIC OF our thoughts through the lens of the false vs true self. The leadership culture that has developed in recent decades is still heavily weighted toward an analytical, intellectual mindset. The reasons for that are many, and we all know that removing emotion from certain business decisions can be essential. But guess what? Thoughts can be just as dangerous in business and elsewhere in life, for one main reason: we can make up whatever thoughts we want. This is a powerful capability that humans have, and it can be used in some positive ways. For now, though, let's explore the ways in which it gets us into trouble.

Let's start with a dramatic example of a movie that portrays a psychopath who justifies harming others because they rationalize, through their thought process, that their victims deserve to be harmed because their victims had previously harmed someone the psychopath cares about. They convince themselves, through logical and rational thought, that their behavior is justified and maybe even honorable. We've all seen characters like this portrayed in movies or books, and while we can see the logic that the character is using, we know, on a much deeper level, that beneath the logic, their behavior is inherently unhealthy and not justifiable at all.

Now apply this pattern to thoughts that we have as leaders daily when making all types of decisions for ourselves and for our organizations and team members. We can easily make up a story, so to speak, in our thoughts that serves to justify a goal that has been developed by the false ego. If the false ego has felt embarrassed by something a team member said at a recent meeting, might we think we are justified in undermining some element of that team member's work to even the score? We can create an ironclad logical argument as to why we should not support that team member based on business analysis, when really, the root of the decision is the embarrassment we felt and the perception that the team member caused. Once we understand the false ego, we can come to understand that no one can make us feel anything—only we can do that to ourselves, so even if their intention was to embarrass, it was our decision to be embarrassed. In this example, aren't we really doing the same thing as the fictional psychopath by deciding from the false ego?

In a leadership culture that is so identified with our thoughts and logical analysis, thoughts can be invented to serve the purposes of our false egos. We must learn how to question our thoughts, understand where they are coming from, and whether they are serving the wrong master. Only when our thoughts are serving our true selves can they lead to sound leadership decisions. When this happens, decisions become easier, and anxiety about having made the right decisions disappears, because our thoughts become aligned with our true selves instead of the false ego.

At this point, you may be thinking: How will I ever improve my decision-making when I must consider my false ego and my false ego-influenced thoughts that justify poor decisions? Think of it like any other business or leadership problem. It can be broken down into manageable pieces with a set of steps to follow. For now, just know that you can get there, and you will be surprised how quickly, if you fully and honestly participate in the steps, you will gain new insight into the influences on your decision-making. From there, you will be able to transcend the influences that don't serve you or your organization.

YOUR TRUE SELF IS
INFINITELY POWERFUL

THE MORE YOU START TO understand the false ego and its control over your life, it becomes tempting to shrug your shoulders and say, "Why bother? It's everywhere! Now that I can see it, I really do understand how it has been running my life. This is too difficult to change. Besides, it's gotten me this far hasn't it?" Consider whether you want to be the puppet or the puppeteer. The reality is what it is, so you might as well step into the role of puppeteer, and take charge of your life, your work, and your outcomes.

Recall that the false ego is never satisfied. As soon as one goal is achieved, it sets another. Setting goals can be a great habit, but not when there is a false ego attachment to the outcome. There needs to be an underlying sense of peace with what is, a measure of trust in the process, and knowledge of your true self that underlies all the goal setting; this way, if a goal is missed or delayed, your sense of self-worth isn't negatively affected.

The true self is not defined by goal achievement. True self-love is love that comes from the true self. It is unconditional love. It loves itself in colossal so-called failures as much as it does when a goal is achieved. The true self can enjoy the achievement of goals, but it will experience joy whether the goal is achieved or not. Can you see the pattern here? The true self is not attached to outcomes in the exterior world. It can engage wholeheartedly in a set of activities based on genuine interest and passion, yet the specific outcome of those activities will not affect the self-love that comes from the true self.

Imagine all the goals, wants, and intended outcomes you have had in the past that didn't go the way you had hoped. Imagine if you could move through those outcomes with no real disappointment or emotional pain. Imagine if you could just dust yourself off and adjust, creating the next goal with the same amount of enthusiasm and passion for the one you just missed. Would your ability to achieve the new goal be higher when working from this mindset? Of course, it would! It would not be held back by the baggage of disappointments, self-judgment, and concern for what others thought of your so-called lack of achievement. None of that would matter. You would be free to bring all your power, skill, and passion to the next goal with no blocks in the way. That is why it is worth embarking on the journey to connect with your true self.

USE WHAT YOU LOVE TO DISCOVER THE TRUE YOU

ONCE YOU START TO SEE your false self, you will start to see it as separate from you. It can help to develop an image in your mind. It may be a circle with a vertical line down the center, with the false you on one side and the true you on the other. It may be a little avatar of the false ego sitting on one shoulder and the true you on the other. Use whatever image feels genuine and natural for you. Having that image will help you to start disengaging from your false ego so that the true you can see it objectively.

When it crops up in a situation, and you realize you were embarrassed, for example, you can say to yourself: "Oh, that was just you, false ego—I see you now." Then it is easy to see that the part of you that can observe your own false ego is the true you. Identifying the false ego and its influence on you daily is the first step to accelerating your connection with your true self.

A good next step is to start musing on what moves you. What do you love to do? Think of the most joyful times in your life. You'll need to muse beyond the often-stated events like the birth of your children or falling in love, to periods of time in your life and specific activities that brought or bring you joy. It's not that major life events aren't important, it's just that they may not be especially useful for connecting with your true self. A great measure of knowing whether you are genuinely enjoying something is when you don't notice the passage of time when you are engaged in the activity. For example, you may have been sailing for hours, but it feels like it's only been thirty minutes. Or you may find that when you paint, your mind is at peace in a way that you are so present that you don't feel the movement of time.

Doing more of what you love ensures a connection with the true you. If the real reason you golf is that it is a great networking vehicle, then be honest with yourself, and let golf be purely for that purpose. Don't convince yourself that you are truly moved by it to justify the time and financial investment in it. After all, what you love and what moves you is a highly personal thing. Nobody can tell you that you love broccoli if you don't, and nobody aside from you, not even your false ego, can tell you what moves you.

A great way to foster this is to simply schedule time with yourself for a personal date each week. This time needs to be completely alone, so that there is no influence from anyone else, even your romantic partner or a close friend. It needs to be all about you, and it needs to be scheduled and respected like any other important appointment in your calendar. It also needs to be something that feels like pure play and not something that needs to get done. It needs to feel indulgent and luxurious and pure fun. If the shed needs painting for example, unless you love to paint walls, that cannot be the activity. The word "should" cannot be part of the process when deciding what to do. What will you do during your date with yourself? As you decide each week on what you are going to do, you will start to see interests emerge and get a sense of what you enjoy. If you already knew, then actually doing them each week helps you to connect with the truth of who you are. Over time, this connection, along with the now conscious identification of the false self, will help you connect more and more with your true self. As you do this, you will notice a greater sense of peace and calm enter your being. This sense of peace will, in turn, create a foundation from which you operate that is far more solid and powerful than the constantly shifting quicksand of the false ego.

EFFORTLESS LEADERSHIP

WHEN THAT SOLID AND POWERFUL foundation is laid, you will not be the only one who notices. Others will notice, either consciously or subconsciously, but they will notice. They will naturally want to know more about you—who you are, what you do, and even why you do it. People will watch your activity and want to emulate elements of what they see in you, whether they are on your team in an organization, potential clients or existing clients, business partners, and so on. Whatever their connection with you, your ability to lead them becomes significantly easier when you are living from the foundation of your true self. They will perceive the strength and power of that foundation and will naturally gravitate toward you.

A word of warning. As you start to make this shift, some people around you may not like it. They are the people who are in your ambient purely because they are engaged with your false self. Their own false egos are codependent with yours, and when you start to reduce the influence of your false ego on your life, they may become uncomfortable with the stronger, more powerful you. They may fall away if they are friends or acquaintances, and this is a healthy development in the long run. You will likely not want to be around them as much either because your new wisdom will see the false ego in them and the codependency, if it is there, between the two of you. This is akin to healthy attrition in an organization, when someone realizes that the job is not right for them and is not in line with their true self, so they choose to find employment elsewhere. Leaders know that kind of turnover is not only healthy but necessary, so that the people who do choose to stay are hopefully fully engaged. It will be the same with team members and others in your ambient as you create that stronger foundation of you.

Chapter 7

THE SWEET RELIEF OF LETTING GO

THE FLAW IN PERFECTIONISM

IF WE ASK TEN LEADERS to describe the perfect solution to a business problem, we could conceivably get ten different answers. Even if there was similarity between some solutions, there would likely be many different ideas about the perfect way to reach the final solution. This reminds us that the idea of perfection really is subjective. Sure, there are certain situations in which perfection is objective, such as having the correct answer to a math problem. Even in math, there are often different ways to derive the final answer, so which way is perfect? That is subjective. So, you can see one flaw in perfectionism: it is subjective. What is perfect to one person is not necessarily perfect to another.

When we are wrapped up in being perfect or creating something perfect, we tend to forget this truth. Perfectionism tends to be hatched by the false ego. We want to be perfect not only to obtain a result but because we want to obtain the approval of others. We want to be perceived a certain way. We want others to think that we are knowledgeable, competent, worthy of a certain title, and so on. Or we want to reduce the chance of being ridiculed or labeled by others. Whatever the reason, the drive to perfection is wrapped up on the false ego's need for the approval and positive perceptions. Now that we see it is really a false ego activity, the flaw in perfectionism really comes to light.

Knowing how subjective it is, you can see how it is even more damaging when we expect perfection from others. As a leader, how can we expect perfection from others when we know the very definition is subjective? The people we are leading will not necessarily have the same definition of perfection, so it is a losing proposition from the beginning. In the end, asking others to be perfect tends to manifest into, "Do it the way I would do it," which is obviously not the way to engage employees. Perfectionism kills our own creativity and the creativity of those we ask it of.

To be clear, I am not saying there is anything wrong with setting high standards for ourselves and others. We can set a goal that is a stretch and set about achieving it while being open to changing the plan along the way as new information arises. We can stay connected to our true selves and not be devastated if the goal isn't achieved.

Setting objectives with team members can be a collaborative process where high standards are set while still allowing for creativity and innovation as to how the final objectives are met. The measurement of that achievement can be an open, honest conversation based on realities that may have arisen after the original goals were defined. This is a constructive and healthy process and is different from demanding perfection either in the final achievement of the goal or in the method in which it is achieved.

THE ILLUSION OF THE BENEFIT OF CONTROL

THE IDEA THAT WE ARE controlling anything more than ourselves is a complete illusion. Further, most of us are not even controlling ourselves, as we have seen with our lack of understanding regarding our true selves and our true nature. True leadership is less about control than most people perceive. Our false egos often initially identify with control freak leaders, who tend also to be perfectionists, and we subconsciously say to ourselves: "They know what they are doing, so I will follow them." If your team members are following your lead in this way, they are not being nearly as engaged, effective, or innovative as they can be, because the false ego codependency has taken hold of the performance dynamic. Consciously or subconsciously, they feel like they are "off the hook," so to speak, because they are just following instructions provided by their leader who they feel has all the control. They are serving the false ego of the leader, who is happy because their false ego is being supported. The problem here is that the team members have become automatons, playing it safe and doing what they are told instead of what they know will create the best result for the organization, based on their experience and research. There is no real accountability and responsibility. So, in the end there is no real benefit to having this so-called control that ultimately yields results that don't tap into the full potential of the team.

Top performers don't like to be micromanaged and controlled, because they know they have something personal and individual to offer that no one else does. They are willing to take the risk of sharing what might ultimately be an idea that is shelved, knowing that the best ideas come out of a process of being open to all ideas, even the ones that turn out to be not worth pursuing.

Great leaders understand this as well and have learned to let go of the illusion of the benefit of controlling others. The true self within a leader can have an objective and a vision, without the need for controlling others in a way that does little more than feed the false ego's need for control. The other amazing thing that happens when leaders let go of this counterproductive control is they feel more secure in their leadership. After all, the false self knows it is built on a shaky foundation, so anything we do to operate more from our true selves feels more comfortable and secure.

TRUST AND CONTROL ARE TWO SIDES OF THE SAME COIN

As MENTIONED IN CHAPTER 2, trust and control are really two sides of the same issue. Trust and control issues are created by—you guessed it—our false ego. When we want to control things we have no business controlling, it is because we want a certain outcome, but more importantly, it is because we don't trust ourselves to deal with an outcome that is not the outcome we wanted. So, we attempt to control the future because we have decided that only one outcome will serve us.

Let's revisit the exercise I mentioned earlier in which I encourage clients to describe the worst possible outcome of whatever they are trying to control. Once they describe it, then I ask, "Now what would you do if that happened?" Invariably, they quickly describe a set of very achievable steps to overcome and address the outcome that they were so desperately trying to avoid. And just like that, they realize that they can overcome the worst outcome they can imagine, should it come to pass. This exercise is simple yet profound when I have clients try it. Suddenly, this seemingly insurmountable outcome that they were trying so hard to avoid is just another outcome that can be navigated. The need for control then diminishes because they now trust themselves to handle whatever happens. Their energies can be more effectively focused on supporting the desired outcome instead of trying to control people and situations to prevent an undesired outcome. It is a shift in perspective and focus.

This lack of trust in ourselves causes us to try to control others. If we are experiencing a lack of trust in ourselves to handle whatever may come, even if this feeling is subconscious, then we end up compensating for this by trying to control things that are really beyond our control. Micromanagers who don't trust anyone to get anything done without their constant involvement need to look inward and ask whether they truly trust themselves. The answer will be no, because their behavior toward others is simply reflecting what they feel about themselves. Refer to the concept of our outer world reflecting our inner world from chapter 1. The work for such leaders is to set about learning to trust themselves so that they can start to trust others and let go of unproductive control.

This concept may seem like a stretch when we are dealing with other people. The logical mind says, "This has nothing to do with me. I have simply assessed that I can't trust this team member to deliver on our action plans." Well, there may indeed be an issue with the team member's performance which needs to be addressed. Some questions to consider are: Do you find that ultimately you don't trust anyone on your team or in your organization to deliver? Is it your style to be controlling when it's not necessary? Most managers understand intellectually that micromanagement isn't healthy, yet team members often report that they feel micromanaged. And therein lies the problem; micromanagers rarely feel that they are micromanagers. As leaders, we often step outside of this intention with the explanation that the behavior is necessary to get the results. This may be effective in the short term, but it is counterproductive in the long run. In business, short-term goals almost always win over long-term goals. We get into this mindset of survival. "If we don't make our numbers this quarter then there won't be a next quarter," is ultimately the thinking that drives this controlling behavior.

On a practical level, the answer is to find a balance between scrutiny of short-term action plans for short-term goals, while providing the space for the longer-term creative thinking with little control. When team members see appropriate amounts of attention being given to these different objectives, they will feel less controlled and know that they are trusted. Once they feel this, having more hands-on input and scrutiny of their short-term goals will not feel as controlling.

Any experienced leader can look back over their career and share examples of when something did not turn out at all as planned and yet ended up having beneficial consequences. This is practical proof that we often forget, which shows us that controlling the outcome is not always as beneficial as we think it is.

TRUST AND CONTROL: THE INFLUENCE OF YOUR PAST

UNRESOLVED PAST EXPERIENCES CAN CREATE trust and control issues. The first instinct for many leaders when they are presented with this idea is to dismiss it, not because they don't see the logical connection but because they decide that while it happens to others it doesn't happen to them. That is because they haven't invested the energy to truly make the connections that are happening subconsciously.

If you perceive, consciously or subconsciously, that it is risky to trust others, then it's not a stretch to consider when, in your past, you trusted someone, and an undesired outcome resulted. It could have been an incident that had nothing to do with business or your career; it could have involved a childhood friend, a parent, or a romantic partner, or you could have judged a decision you made and therefore don't trust yourself. We tend to compartmentalize these experiences so that we neglect to see the connections between events that are real and are influencing us. Remember my story from chapter 1, regarding bullying when I was a child that later affected my ability to be my best in my business.

Even when we do acknowledge the influence of the past, we tend to stop at the mere intellectual exercise of concluding that the connections are logical. We say, "Oh yes, that makes perfect sense," and then move on with our day. If we want to ensure that we're not being affected, though, it takes an extra level of effort to look at leadership and business problems in a new way. We must bring ourselves into the equation. When we are looking at a business issue, we must include the introspection about ourselves to consider questions such as: "What is my bias here?" "Have I seen this kind of thing happen in a similar way before—that is, is there a pattern in my ambient that I should be paying attention to?" and "What events have been a part of this pattern?"

The other reason we stop at the intellectual acknowledgment of the influence of our past on trust and control issues is that our false ego quickly decides that we have already dealt with and let go of our past. It decides that if we were to acknowledge that something in our past is still affecting us, we are weak or "less than" in some way. The irony is, of course, that to be open to the truth about ourselves is the strongest thing we can do as leaders. Once we do this a few times, we can see the benefit, and our ability to lead becomes easier as we resolve our own internal issues.

THE TRUE YOU HAS NO ATTACHMENT TO OUTCOME

IN THE CONTEXT OF LETTING go, it can be helpful to revisit the attachment to outcome covered earlier. The question that inevitably comes up when I challenge clients to let go of control and attachment to outcome is: How can I let go of the attachment to a certain outcome when that is what I am measured on? There is a delicate but essential dance that needs to happen between goal setting and emotional attachment to the goal being achieved. Of course, we need to be clear on the goal and develop an action plan to achieve it, then execute that action plan. And the key shift in mindset that needs to happen is this: even though we have decided to work hard toward executing on the action plan, we remain emotionally grounded in the knowledge that the achievement of the goal does not affect who we are, how worthy we are, or how we feel about ourselves. We do the work in the external world, yes, but we are not emotionally attached to the outcome. It's this separation that true leaders need to learn because without the emotional weight of attachment to the outcome, we are infinitely more effective! That is the paradox.

There are many examples in sport where this is evident. We have heard countless interviews with winners of the most elite competitions when they say things such as, "I just decided to do my best and have fun," or "I just let go and decided to enjoy being here at this level of competition." As spectators, when we know the team or athletes we are watching, we can often tell when they are "tight"—when they have not found their flow because of the so-called pressure of the situation. We see it readily in sports like golf. The winner on any given day is typically the one who stays loose, stays in the flow, and stays in the right mindset of being focused and yet relaxed and detached at the same time. At the elite level, any one of many players can win on any given day; they all have enough skill on a physical level to win. But the person who best connects with the right mindset will win. This is the same mindset I am referring to, that great leaders need to connect with within themselves.

You might be wondering, "If my true self is not attached to the outcome, then how can it have a purpose? Wouldn't it be attached to the outcomes associated with that purpose?" To clarify, we need to make a distinction between the purpose and the outcome. You may know that your purpose is to be a defense lawyer, but your true self does not need to be attached to winning every single case.

THERE IS NO SUCH THING AS STRESS

STRESS IS A WORD WE use so often as if it is a core feeling. It has become a catch-all term used to describe other, more fundamental feelings that need to be processed so that we can let them go. Think of any situation in which you would describe yourself as feeling stressed. Then name the core feelings underlying the stress. Are you feeling anger, hurt, fear, anxiety, guilt, shame, jealousy, sadness, loss, grief, something else, or a combination of these emotions?

Letting go is about processing your feelings fully and completely. The reason they tend to pile up to the point that we feel "stress" is that we bury them, ignore them, meditate, or even talk about them, but don't fully process them. To process a feeling, we must first lean into it—feel it! If you don't believe that this is a sound approach, recall how young children process their emotions.

Imagine a three-year-old wants to go outside to play, but they are not given permission. The child feels "stress" in not being allowed to do what they want to do. Perhaps they feel angry and sad. First, they throw a tantrum with every fiber of their being. They express themselves verbally and loudly, with feelings obviously reflected in the body. The child's body position may become rigid, or they express anger physically by stamping their feet, throwing things, lashing out, and so on. Their body temperature might even rise a bit. Then, the child might become sad and cry. They are processing feelings in a very complete way—verbally, by crying, physically through the body, and through specific actions. We know it is happening because we witness it. And here is the point: at the end of the tantrum and the crying, the child often moves on to another item of interest as if nothing had happened. The reason they can be singing and happily playing a few minutes after a tantrum is that the child has fully processed the emotions they were feeling. There is simply nothing left to do with those emotions.

A note on meditation. While meditation is beneficial, don't confuse it with processing emotions. Meditation is about emptying the mind or just observing thoughts with a level of objectivity, so it is obviously different from leaning into emotions. Ideally meditation is best used in addition to emotional processing. Imagine how much better your meditation will be after you have fully processed whatever emotions had been causing you to feel "stressed."

So how do we, as adults, process our emotions fully without having tantrums and throwing things? We deploy methods to fully process emotions without impacting or harming others. What does this have to do with leadership and letting go of control? When we are not walking around with days, weeks, months, or years of unprocessed emotions, the trust and control issues have less sway on our way of operating in the world. When we are at peace internally and aren't feeling stressed, we can more easily see the ability of others to contribute and perform. We have clarity.

Chapter 8
FROM COLLABORATION TO CONNECTION

THE WHOLE IS IN EACH PART

YOU HAVE PROBABLY HEARD THE familiar phrase, "The whole is greater than the sum of its parts." In successful relationships, that is true. The interaction between two or more people can create something so much greater than just the individual contributions added together.

Looking at this concept in a deeper way, the whole is also *within* each part. There is really no separation between individuals except for the ones we perceive. What if we created a culture where connection without agenda, false ego, and unhealthy competition could thrive?

The value of collaboration is generally accepted in today's corporate environments. We have reduced physical walls between employees, flattened organization structures, and become more agile in our way of working—all to encourage collaboration. What if we focused a little deeper on creating the space for true connection between the individuals doing the collaborating? When we collaborate, we share intellectual ideas, but do we share anything related to our true selves?

Instead of just getting along, what if leaders created a culture that allowed meaningful connection? And why bother? Because connection takes collaboration to a whole new level. Connection speaks to a deeper human need that goes beyond a work task or a deadline. If leveraged, connection fosters greater innovation and creativity than collaboration alone. The intention here is to allow employees to be the full human beings that they are, in the context of work.

We tend to compartmentalize ourselves in the different roles in our lives—CEO, spouse, parent, sibling, child—as if we are split into these roles. While it can be helpful to step in and out of these roles for the purposes of accomplishing different things, an individual is one connected, single being. There is value in bringing our whole selves to the conversation, meeting, or interaction. With this type of connection, we collaborate as a whole human being, not as a person who is playing a role for a specific project. This creates a much richer experience and establishes a true connection between teammates that allows for greater creativity and a more fruitful collaboration.

YOUR RELATIONSHIP AMBIENT

IN CHAPTER 1, I EXPLAINED how the things that happen in our ambient reflect our inner world. Our relationships are simply part of that ambient, whether they are personal connections or work relationships. Look for the patterns in your relationships, such as the victimization pattern mentioned in the first chapter.

It might be surprising to realize that you can access character traits that you admire in others. A simple tool for doing this: list the trait you admire in the person. Get really clear on it—picture it if it helps. If you invest some time thinking about it, you can likely come up with a few situations in which you demonstrated that trait. Examine what enabled you to demonstrate that trait at the time and then how you could access that part of you again.

Perhaps even more surprising is that the traits you tend to really dislike in others are within you as well. Think Law of Similars here: what bothers you about others tends to be what, on some level, bothers you about yourself. This can be a hard pill to swallow, but admitting this is a powerful method of connecting more deeply with the people in your ambient.

Think of an example of a trait that you really dislike in someone else. If you are totally honest with yourself, you can probably think of a time that you behaved similarly. Perhaps your actions were not as extreme, but some action or thought was like what you observed in the other person. Recall how you felt when you had that thought or took that action. It is probably quite similar to how you feel when someone else displays that behavior.

So how can you leverage this knowledge? First, admitting that you possess a trait that you don't like to see in others provides a bridge to the person of whom you are being critical. You can have new compassion for that individual because you have compassion for yourself, do you not? And you have just concluded that the two of you have something in common, right? Naturally, this will allow for a deeper connection with that individual, born through the realization that you are not as different from them as you originally thought.

WENDY KNIGHT AGARD

Taking this one step further, you can leverage this understanding to evolve your own leadership ability and character structure. If you pay attention to what really bothers you about someone else and apply the Law of Similars as we have here, you can then set about improving on that character trait within you. For example, let's say you perceive a pattern of a team member being selfish in their approach to taking credit for team achievement. Can you think of a time when you acted similarly? How did it feel when you did? Was there some guilt about doing it? How would you like to change that behavior? What can you do right now, tomorrow, or the next time a similar opportunity arises? Can you see how this internal reflection challenges you to evolve your own ability to lead?

THE FALSE EGO AND RELATIONSHIPS

ONE OF THE EASIEST WAYS to spot the influence of the false ego is through relationship dynamics. Are you comparing yourself to others? Do you feel a sense of competition that is not directly and solely attributed to a business requirement to compete? As a leader of others, do you feel that you need to know more about the topics than those who report to you know, even when it is their subject of expertise? If the answer to any of these questions is yes, the false ego is at play and will negatively affect your relationship with your team.

Consider a more subtle example. Perhaps you feel envious when a peer receives accolades or a promotion. What is engaging the false ego here? The question to ask yourself is: If I were aligned with my true self, clear on my intentions, and doing work that was meaningful, would my false ego be comparing my progress to that of others? The obvious answer is no. Knowing this creates a space to get your false ego in check and genuinely be happy with your colleague's success. Conversely, not acknowledging this will undoubtedly have a negative effect on the relationship with your colleague.

COMMUNICATING WHAT YOU NEED

INTELLIGENT, COMPETENT, AND KNOWLEDGEABLE WORKERS want to connect to their work. When people have a thorough understanding of why something is being asked of them, their commitment to the task grows. The *why* must be more than "because the vice president wants us to." A context for the request needs to be communicated on several levels—the team, the organization, the competitive landscape, and so on. When this is done well, team members feel part of the process and can fully support the request.

To take this a level deeper, being vulnerable creates a deeper connection still. Admitting that you feel anxious about the implications of not completing the task well or on time, for example—admitting that there are elements of what is required that you don't understand—creates a level of cocreation that moves beyond mere collaboration.

ASSUMPTIONS ARE THE FALSE EGO SAYING, "I KNOW"

ASSUMPTIONS ARE THE LAZY WAY out for the mind. If we assume, based on what has been done before, on a directive from a higher level within the organization, or for any other reason, this is just the false ego wanting the comfort of thinking it knows all the answers without having to make the effort to find out what the answers are. This applies whether we are making assumptions about ourselves or our teams.

The first question to ponder here is, Do you even know what you want? Really? Or are you leading based on objectives that have been handed down to you, without thinking about what you want your personal or team contribution to be—and assuming that is all you really want? It's easy to assume that you know what you want based on assumptions made by the false ego. But what about the deeper ideas, the deeper meaning, the deeper change of which you would like to be part? Get clear on this for yourself before you try to engage your team.

You can't assume your team members know what you want either, even if you are clear on it. Likewise, you can't assume you know what your team members want. A common assumption that I have seen in organizations is the definition of what it means to an individual to excel. Managers often assume that they know what the definition of growth is for their team members, without asking the team members how they themselves define their own development.

QUIET CONNECTION

CONNECTION DOES NOT HAVE TO come from actions that are easy to observe, such as motivational talks, having regular one-on-one conversations, or other obvious efforts. It can come from a more subtle place that is not as easy to see in a physical sense, yet it can be just as powerful and effective. This is where authenticity comes into play. The stereotype of the leader as extrovert, with great public-speaking skills, is not the only type of leader that can create connection.

Invest time to get to know who you are at the core, when no one is watching, when you are not trying to deliver on objectives set by others, and when you are not trying to meet expectations of others. If you allow this knowing to permeate your leadership activities, others will sense this authenticity and connection will be created with little effort because human beings, at their core, just want to be themselves. When you are yourself, others will feel comfortable being themselves in your presence, and you will both naturally be more open to true connection.

Chapter 9
THE POWER IN VULNERABILITY

WHY VULNERABILITY IS POWERFUL

IN RECENT YEARS, THE IDEA of vulnerability being part of leadership has become more popular. This is happening because we are starting to realize that the habit of creating a leadership persona and compartmentalizing ourselves so that we only allow our perceived strengths to be seen is not the most effective way to connect with the people we are leading. Leadership is about connection, and connection happens powerfully through vulnerability.

We love to cheer for the underdog in competitions, yet we try to hide it when we are the underdog. Why not have those that we are leading cheer for us? When you ask people who report to you for help in a way that demonstrates vulnerability, they naturally want to do what they can to help, and the whole team succeeds. A connection gets created that is personal and authentic.

SELF-LOVE

BEING VULNERABLE IN FRONT OF others demonstrates a level of acceptance of yourself. You are saying, "Hey, I feel overwhelmed here, and even though I don't like feeling that way, I accept that I do, so much so that I am willing to share this with others." That kind of acceptance speaks to self-love and is worth revisiting in the context of vulnerability.

We are so hard on ourselves as we navigate the challenges of life that over time the internal critic can dominate many of our thoughts. How many times have you heard your internal voice call yourself an idiot, stupid, loser, or some other harsh term you would never call someone else? Yet somehow, we have decided it's all right to call ourselves these derogatory names and judge ourselves more harshly than we judge others.

One exercise I have often given coaching clients is to stand in front of a full-length mirror, completely nude, without makeup or jewelry, look themselves in the eye and say, "I love you," several times out loud. For many of us, it is not an easy exercise and stimulates some interesting self-discovery. Doing this in the nude is not about making peace with your physical body, (although it could be a valuable side bonus); it is about stripping away any physical "armor" that creates a separation between you and your reflection.

Learning to love ourselves, even when we are experiencing emotions that we judge as negative, can be a process that takes some time. Practicing vulnerability is a great way to accelerate this process because, as mentioned above, it demonstrates a level of acceptance of ourselves, even in a challenging situation.

LYING THOUGHTS: THE TRUTH OF EMOTIONS

REMEMBER THE LINK BETWEEN THOUGHTS and the brain-mind, or intellect, which is linked to the false ego. Then recall the scenario shared earlier, in which the false ego leads you to feel jealous of a colleague. That jealousy can easily influence the intellect to create a situation in your mind where this colleague is deliberately trying to undermine you at work, when in fact that is not happening. This type of thinking happens so much more often than we realize, until we learn how to identify and process our emotions.

Some will say that our thoughts influence our emotions more often than the other way around. Who's to say which happens more often, but the direction from emotion to thought is more valuable to recognize, because emotions are more likely to be true. Remember that we can convince ourselves of anything in our intellect, as it is run by the false ego much of the time.

You might be wondering: *Well, if the false ego caused you to feel jealous in the first place, then it influences the feeling just as much as the thought, so why are feelings more "true" than thoughts?* The answer is that even though the source might be the false ego, emotions are more difficult to fake than thoughts. If you are feeling jealous, it is difficult to just instantly stop being jealous, because the feeling is "true." The scenario of the colleague undermining you could be totally false and yet is easily created by your thoughts. If feelings were easy to "fake," then depression, anxiety, and the like wouldn't be so common, because people could easily just change their emotions. We know that changing an emotion just because we want to is very difficult, but making up a story in our heads with thought is so easy we don't even realize when we are doing it much of the time. Because of this, being vulnerable enough to acknowledge our emotions is essential for strong leadership.

You can see, then, how acknowledging emotions also provides clarity.

In the scenario described above, if your first conscious thought is, *My colleague is constantly doing things to undermine me*, and you stop there, you have a problem with no resolution. If, however, you ask yourself, "How does this situation make me feel?" and the answer is jealous, now you are aware that you feel jealous. Then if you understand that only the false ego can feel jealous, you can question the thought you have about your colleague because you can question whether that thought was triggered by the jealousy that you are feeling. Going forward, you may be able to look at the whole situation with more clarity and might even draw a different conclusion. Perhaps you will determine that actually you are just jealous, and they are not doing anything to undermine you. This understanding is incredibly powerful when you practice it and apply it more and more to conclusions you have drawn with your thinking. This process is humbling, and once you start to do it, it will be easier to be vulnerable because you will be in closer touch with your emotions.

THE IMPORTANCE OF
PROCESSING EMOTIONS

So, ONCE YOU START TO become aware of your emotions, then what do you do about them? We already spoke about how difficult it is to just flip a switch on emotions that you are feeling deeply. The answer is to feel them fully. To process them fully. Our tendency is to suppress emotions that we judge as negative. Note that it is only our own judgment that decides whether an emotion is good or bad. Our true selves simply feel the emotion with no judgment. Only the false ego will judge it as positive or negative. Understanding this idea is not intended to minimize the intensity of what you are experiencing. For example, someone suffering from clinical depression may be at a point where applying these ideas on their own is not an adequate approach to treatment. The point is to provide insight on where the emotion comes from and how to process it.

Processing an emotion is a bit like processing the food we take in. We must accept it, "chew on it," so to speak, and feel it fully. Suppressing it and trying to pretend it is not there is a bit like swallowing a piece of meat whole, without chewing, and expecting it to digest easily. The chewing starts pre-digestion to make it easier for the gut to do its work. Applying a different analogy, it's like steering into a skid when you are driving. Our instinct is to overcorrect away from the skid, which is more likely to make things worse. But steering into the skid for just a moment provides a greater possibility of coming out of it safely. It is the same with emotions; we need to steer into them for a bit, to feel them fully, to let them go. Recall the example of the three-year-old having a tantrum. Young children instinctively know how to fully process their emotions. We gradually lose this ability as we age, and we're taught to start suppressing them instead of being provided with ways to process them without negatively impacting others.

A STEP-BY-STEP GUIDE TO PROCESSING EMOTIONS

LET'S REVISIT THE IDEA OF processing emotions by bringing together all of the ideas we have explored so far. The first step to processing emotions is learning to name them. It is important to get clear on which feeling is most present, and start from there. Once you start defining them, you will often find that there are several emotions playing out at once. Don't be alarmed; just make a note of each one, and apply this exercise to each one, one at a time.

One way to help name specific emotions is to think of them in rough categories as follows: grief/loss/sadness/hurt/despair, anger/frustration, fear/anxiety/panic, guilt/shame/jealousy. It can be helpful, after naming the first emotion that comes to mind, to ask yourself what the feeling behind that initial emotion is. For example, anger is often the "surface emotion" to what is really hurt. When we are hurt, we often react first with anger, because being angry feels less vulnerable than feeling hurt. Even if you discover this underlying emotion, invest the time to process both, and start with the first one you become aware of.

Now that you have a list of emotions, find a quiet, private space to sit or lie down where you can be comfortable and relaxed. Close your eyes. To help center your attention, it helps to deploy a physical habit, such as placing a few fingers in the dip in the center of your chest. Do this now, then start by saying a phrase of self-acceptance out loud, to remind yourself that it is okay to be feeling this emotion, such as: "Even though I have this feeling of (whatever emotion you have identified), I love and accept all aspects of myself." If you have never said words like this about yourself out loud, this may feel awkward, silly, or even untrue. If it is a challenge, then just complete this step for several days in a row until it feels less awkward. You don't need to feel that you fully believe it to say it. Just allow for the possibility that some day you might believe it.

Once you have become more comfortable with this initial step, move your fingers to the orbit of your eye, just above your nose. Now think about the feeling you named. If you are visually oriented, see the word in your mind's eye. If you are auditory-oriented, hear the word internally. Now sink into the feeling of the emotion. Imagine you are in a bath full of that emotion. Imagine you are swimming in that emotion. Imagine it is all around you; it is in every single individual cell in your body. Each cell is teeming with that emotion. Imagine your body is vibrating with that emotion. For these few moments, this emotion is all you know. It is everything. You breathe that emotion in, and you exhale it. When you feel fully emerged in the feeling, then make it even bigger, more dramatic, and more intense than it really was when you started. Imagine you are making a movie and dramatizing the whole thing. Continue to make it bigger and more intense, until it feels like there is nothing left—like a shift has happened, and perhaps a new thought or feeling comes to mind.

Notice that new feeling, then bring your fingers back to the center of your chest. Start the process all over again with the new feeling or thought. Use the same phrase but insert the new feeling or thought as you say it out loud. Once you feel an acceptance of that feeling or thought, move your fingers to the orbit of your eye again, and repeat the process of feeling the emotion fully, magnifying and exaggerating it until there is nothing left to feel. Observe what new feeling or thought arises at the end of that step. Repeat the whole process with the new emotion.

At some point, the emotions or thoughts that start to arise will become more positive. You will gain a new perspective and will eventually have a feeling of peace, warmth, and calm that comes to mind. When you get to that point, repeat the process with this new, enjoyable feeling, until it feels that there is nothing left to process. You will know when you reach this point. You will just know. Then take a few moments before opening your eyes and coming back into the room. Feel your body against the surface it is on, start to wiggle your toes, notice your breathing, take a few deep breaths—then slowly and deliberately, bring your focus and attention to the here and now and finally, open your eyes and coming fully into the present.

A few notes about this exercise:

- Don't worry about doing it perfectly. It is just a starting point to help you practice steering into the skid of your feelings so that you can process them. It is a simplified version of work I have done with clients and training I received from Satyen Raja. If you have experienced another method, such as journaling, and that works for you, then incorporate that method into a regular routine.

- This process is not a substitute for professional counseling or coaching. As with any emotional issue, if the issue is persistent and/or affects your life in a significant way, seek the support of a professional.

- Processing an emotion once does not mean you will never feel it again. If it is in relation to a specific issue, you may find that the feelings dissipate over time if you practice processing them. Think of it like an upward spiral. You may come back around to the same feeling about the same situation, but you will have let go of a little more of it each time. It is like training for a sport; you can't practice a skill once and expect not to have to do it again. Even elite athletes invest a significant amount of time in practicing. Sometimes, their skill seems like it is deteriorating a little as they learn a new element in their sport, but once they master it, their overall capability improves. Likewise, when you are vulnerable enough to fully feel your emotions, you might feel a little worse off than you did when you were suppressing them because you are not used to really feeling them. You will, however, come through it stronger, happier, and wiser than you were before. Recall the happy three-year-old after a tantrum. Are they not evolving and learning because of their tantrum? Of course, they are. They are learning to feel, to express, to deal with not getting what they want and so on. They take this learning and evolve. In effect, this exercise is a controlled, internal tantrum of sorts. You are feeling the feeling fully and intensely to move through it until it dissipates.

- Over time, if you practice it, you will become better and better at processing your emotions. You will be able to identify them more precisely and process them faster. You may get to the point where all you have to do is recognize the emotion, and then you find yourself saying, "Ah, I know what this is. Let me just take a few seconds to feel it. I know that I can move through it quickly," and by the time you say that sentence to yourself, you have processed the emotion and moved on to whatever you need to do next. You will find yourself doing this in real time at work and in your personal life. You can see how this can then become part of your daily life and how powerful and freeing it can be to be moving through life without carrying around the baggage of piles of unprocessed emotions.

THE ANGER GAME

THIS EXERCISE HAS BEEN SHARED with me by intuitive healer, counselor, and teacher Shelley Kabelin and is a powerful reflection of the Law of Similars that was introduced in chapter 1. Imagine that you are angry with a coworker. The first step is to name the emotion and accept it and the part of yourself that is feeling it, like the first step of the emotional processing exercise in the previous section. Write the following statement: "I love the part of me that is angry." Then, get clear on why you are angry. For example, write "I love the part of me that is angry with my coworker for treating me with disrespect." Now the third step is the challenge. Deploying the idea that outer reflects inner, write this third statement: I love the part of me that is angry with *myself* for treating me with disrespect.

By now, you know what the exercise here is about. Ask yourself in what recent situations you have not been respecting yourself. If you can sit in this vulnerability for a while, you will undoubtedly become aware of a behavior or habit that you have engaged in that you know on some level wasn't respecting yourself. The personal situation does not have to be directly related to the situation you observed in someone else's actions—it is simply the nature of the action that will be similar. So, if disrespect is the issue you are upset about, look for situations in which you disrespected yourself. If not feeling heard is the issue you are upset about, look for situations in which you didn't listen to yourself.

To demonstrate, let me relate an example of a time that I used this tool on myself. My husband and I took our girls for a drive to a small town outside of the city. We stopped for a bite to eat on the way home. As I was looking at the menu, there wasn't much that appealed to me, and I had some food sensitivities that I needed to be mindful of at the time. My order arrived with fries, which I had no intention of eating. Then, as often happens with things like fries sitting on a plate, I decided to just have a few. They really weren't particularly good fries; they were tasteless and greasy, but I found myself unconsciously finishing most of them. At the end of the meal, I had that bloated brick-in-the-stomach feeling.

We left the restaurant, and as we started to pull away on the highway, we realized that one of us forgot our gloves in the restaurant. We were on a two-lane highway, and so I expected my husband to pull over, then do a U-turn, and go back to the restaurant. What he did instead was reverse backward down the highway. At one point, he swerved a bit because he was driving faster than you normally drive in reverse. There were no other cars on this quiet country highway, but the swerve was a little unnerving. I became very angry about what I considered to be him exercising poor judgment, and we argued about it.

After we picked up the gloves and were back on the highway, I noticed how angry I still was and walked myself through this exercise. What I realized, once I got to step three, is that I was angry at myself for exercising poor judgment—about eating the fries! So even though I was upset about the driving decision, I was angrier about that than I needed to be, because I was really angry at myself for eating those fries.

FROM CAN'T TO WON'T TO WILL

ONE ELEMENT OF BEING VULNERABLE is being willing to admit how much of our lives are influenced by our own choices. It is a level of responsibility that many of us shy away from because it is easier to explain away situations by looking outside of ourselves to causes that we tell ourselves are beyond our control.

A powerful exercise that I developed for coaching clients to demonstrate the power of choice is the can't/won't/will exercise. First, think of something you have heard yourself say that you can't do. I am not talking about saying that you can't play in the NBA when you are sixty years old, because that is very likely true, and being vulnerable to the truth of the choices you are making is probably not going to change it. Recall an everyday conclusion you have drawn, such as, "I can't talk to that team member about their poor performance."

Here are the steps:

Write down the statement: "I can't talk to that team member about the issue I have with their performance." Then, write the statement again, directly below the first sentence, but replace the word *can't* with *won't*, so now that statement reads, "I *won't* talk to that team member about the issue I have with their performance." It has just become painfully obvious that you have made a choice, consciously or unconsciously, not to speak to that team member. This realization is powerful because there are so many *can't* statements that we say to ourselves every day, preventing us from achieving what we want to achieve. The vulnerability of admitting this is particularly helpful for rooting out decisions you are making unconsciously about what you can or cannot do. The final step is to replace the word *won't* with *will* if the statement is something you have been wanting to do.

Vulnerability plays out in a few ways in this example. Admitting the truth to yourself that you have made a choice about something that you had told yourself you couldn't do is one vulnerable element. The action itself of speaking to the team member you are having difficulty with is likely, also, a vulnerable action, and the original thought that you couldn't do it was likely more about this vulnerability than it was about a lack of skill or any other factors.

This is one of the issues with so much of the leadership training that happens in organizations. The focus is on skill, but skill will not be applied if the underlying issues of vulnerability, beliefs, the false ego, and the other topics covered in this book are not addressed. These topics need to be addressed first because they are the foundation that prepares the individual to easily learn and, most importantly, apply the skills they learn.

Chapter 10
DIVERSITY, INCLUSION, AND BELONGING FROM THE INSIDE OUT

AN INSIDE LOOK

WHEN I STARTED THIS BOOK several years ago, diversity was not a hot topic. It was hovering there, as it had been for the previous ten or twenty years, as a topic of leadership and employee engagement discussions in the world of organizational development, team dynamics, and so on. As is often the case, it took the awareness of some events that happened to famous people (the sexual harassment and assault cases that occurred in the entertainment industry) for this topic to land where it needed to be all along—front and center on the agenda of senior leaders. The heightened attention given to recent cases of antiblack racism in the United States has further pushed people out of their slumber when it comes to this topic. For those who still didn't believe in or understand the importance of the issue, they have had to deal with it to manage the perception of employees, customers, and partners—they have had to show they were doing something to address it or risk being perceived as part of the problem.

So here we are, looking at a topic that has always been as important as it is now, with a new lens of urgency and managing perceptions. Now that everyone is talking about diversity, inclusion, and belonging, let's try looking at it from a different point of view: you.

If we think about the Law of Similars mentioned in chapter 1, we can apply it here to the topic of diversity, inclusion, and belonging. When we start to understand, embrace, and even develop diversity within ourselves, we will naturally do this in our external world. The human tendency to fear or judge those who are different from us is one of the core issues affecting our ability to accept others. If we can start to see ourselves as the many-faceted and diverse beings that we are, this inner belief will be reflected in our actions in the world outside of ourselves.

What does this have to do with leadership? As I have said before, leadership of others starts with leadership of yourself—it is leadership from the inside out. Begin the process of looking within to notice how you are in different situations. For example, we tend to compartmentalize our lives and accept this as healthy; we behave a certain way on vacation versus at work, with our spouse versus friends, and so on. What about comparing how you were when you were ten years old versus how you are now? This idea might sound ridiculous at first glance because our intellect concludes that we would naturally be vastly different because of maturity and life experiences. But have you ever examined the more nuanced elements of who you were at that age, before puberty, before the responsibilities and demands of life affected you? What did you love to do? I often use this question in coaching conversations for clients who are looking for a career change and/or looking for more purpose and meaningful work. You would be surprised how helpful that simple exercise is for reminding people about the parts of themselves they have left behind for all sorts of practical and logical reasons that have now led to a disconnection with important parts of themselves.

Learning to stay connected with those important parts of ourselves—the parts that give our lives meaning, the parts that bring pure joy simply for the sake of experiencing joy—is a valuable tool for creating a space of inclusion within ourselves for ourselves. This type of internal work is essential if we want to create truly inclusive cultures in organizations, because if we can't accept the diversity within ourselves, then our ability to truly embrace others is compromised.

BEYOND ASSESSMENTS

MANY OF US HAVE COMPLETED assessment surveys at work that provide insight into our behaviors and motivations. These assessment tools can be helpful, but it is important not to accept your initial assessment results as a fixed state that you cannot change. These assessment tools should be viewed as a starting point for growth and development as opposed to a tool for explaining or predicting behavior. This may go against theories that encourage you to just focus on playing to your strengths. As mentioned in chapter 2, leveraging strengths can be beneficial, but growth happens when you stretch to develop new skills and demonstrate new ways of being. The goal should be to evolve to a way of being that makes it difficult for others to guess what your "type" might be, because they see you accessing skills and behaviors from many "types" within whatever model they are considering.

ACCEPT, EMBRACE AND DEVELOP DIVERSITY WITHIN

BEING OPEN TO DIVERSITY WITHIN ourselves might sound easy, but it takes conscious and consistent effort. How many times have you heard your inner voice say things like, "I am not creative," or "I would love to do that job, but I am not good at one of the core skills needed to perform well in that position," "I want to move forward in my career, but I am an introvert, so I am not comfortable highlighting my achievements to others," and the like. The key is to separate your natural tendencies from your skills. People tend to conflate these two parameters, but they don't need to be conflated and shouldn't be if you want to develop as a leader and as one who embraces diversity and inclusiveness.

And this internal diversity is so much more than tendencies and skills; it's accepting the diversity of moods, interests, likes, dislikes, and behaviors that you have. Recall from chapter 8 that if you dislike something about yourself, chances are you dislike that same trait when you see it in others. So now, you have a conscious or unconscious bias against this stranger, simply because they remind you of a part of yourself that you dislike! Imagine if we all developed such a deep sense of self-love that we could embrace all of ourselves, even when there are parts that we want to change and improve. Imagine how that would manifest in increased compassion, acceptance, and love for others. Imagine how much more open we would be in our leadership styles and how much more inclusive we would be in hiring and giving opportunities to others.

We also tend to dislike the parts of ourselves that we judge as weaknesses. So, if I feel that I am weak when it comes to dealing with conflict at work, I am likely to dislike that about myself. Now if I am interviewing someone, and I perceive that the interviewee is also weak in that area, I will allow my bias to affect my ability to see this person clearly and reject them because the person reminds me of a part of myself that I don't like. You might be thinking, *Yes, but if the candidate is like me, then wouldn't I hire them because people tend to hire others who are like themselves?* When we hire people who are like us, what we really mean is that they are like us in the areas we like about ourselves, not in the areas we don't like. You can see how this can really make achieving diversity and inclusion a challenge, because the truth is that we have many unconscious insecurities and things we don't like about ourselves that are playing out in our interactions.

What is your personal brand of genius? What unique talents and gifts do you feel you have, including those talents that others may not really be aware of and that haven't shown up on assessments tests? Revel in knowing that you have this personal brand of genius for a moment. Really acknowledge how great you are and these things that you love about yourself. Now take a few moments to think about the things that have typically presented a challenge for you—the things that you would really love to change about yourself that you don't like about yourself. Notice how your mood changed when you started to think about the second category of things about yourself. Your mood likely took a turn for the worse. Imagine if you could embrace the latter category of traits and skills the same way you embraced the elements that you feel make up your personal brand of genius. How would that affect your judgment of someone else who displays those same character traits? If you could truly embrace the parts of yourself that you don't like or judge as inferior, you would likely be more open to embracing those traits in others.

Recall the emotional processing exercise in chapter 9. Even when we are experiencing an emotion that we judge as negative, we start the process with a statement that says, "I love, accept, and respect the part of me that is feeling the emotion." When I have worked with coaching clients to guide them in this type of visualization, often just saying that sentence out loud moves them to tears. They have never taken a moment to accept and love emotions that they judge as bad or unwanted. Imagine if we used this statement with all aspects of ourselves, even the ones we don't like or want to improve. As we have learned, this self-acceptance is a vital first step to change and improvement anyway. It is much more difficult to improve on something that you dislike, suppress, and ignore. The position of judgement creates a barrier to being able to improve and to create the separation I mentioned earlier. You are not your skills and abilities. This is another way of creating a healthy separation. You are still you whether you can ride a bicycle or not. This is so easy to accept if you don't have a strong desire to learn to ride a bicycle in this moment, yet when it comes to things we have a desire for, or that we don't like about ourselves, we fail to make this simple (albeit not easy) separation.

One objection I often hear from coaching clients in underrepresented groups is "I don't want to have to behave in ways that feel inauthentic to get ahead. I want to be myself. Why can't the business environment accept me for who I am and give me the same opportunities to advance?" So they are stuck, because they want the opportunities, but they are hoping and waiting for others to change. Now imagine if they could make the separation between their nature and their skills that I mentioned earlier. Imagine if they could really accept that being weak in the required skill is perfectly all right and has nothing to do with who they are. Now imagine that they can see that skill like learning to ride a bicycle—a simple skill that does not reflect on their authenticity or personality one way or the other— it is just skill that they can master should they choose to master it. You can see, then, that they are more likely to develop the skill coming from this open mind and place of self-love than trying to move the mountain of hating themselves for not being good at it and hating the environment for expecting them to be. Think of it like going on a trip to a place you've never been. You are still you, still authentic; you're just trying something new to expand your world. The leadership here is happening from the inside out: the internal thoughts and feelings shift first and provide a foundation for the desired outcome to manifest in the external world.

Of course, it is also important for organizations to create an inclusive culture where everyone can bring their whole selves to work and feel comfortable being who they are and being authentic. If individuals focused on the kind of internal development that I described earlier in conjunction with improvements in organizational culture, we would experience better and faster results in our collective desire to embrace others as they are and be embraced as we are.

AFTERWORD

Leadership is hard. It requires constant growth. As soon as you think you have figured it out, a situation or team member will come into your ambient and challenge what you thought you knew. You won't get it right every time. You will experience situations that feel like failure.

But you can recover from the difficult times and feel a measure of peace despite the challenges *if* you are willing to invest the time and energy to lead from the inside out so that you can access your own personal brand of genius—your *Everyday Genius*.

Peace.

Wendy

ACKNOWLEDGEMENTS

What a strange and challenging process it has been to try to make sense of a series of thoughts, feelings, and connections in my head and body-mind. This book was 90 percent finished in 2015, so to finally create space in my life to come back to it and complete it has been a rewarding process that has brought a sense of peace.

Thank you to Junior, who never questioned that I would complete this book even though I did. Thank you to my daughter Mackenzie Agard for patiently working through multiple rounds of edits as well as publishing and marketing work as I jumped in and out of this project over time. Thank you to my daughter Bailey for her marketing support and for reminding me through her example that there is always time to squeeze in something else that I want to do.

Being in the right frame of mind to finally finish this work has been facilitated by my fabulous coaching colleagues at Shopify, who have welcomed me and created space for me to be in flow more often, which in turn, created the mental space and energy to write on weekends and during vacation days.

I would also like to thank the numerous coaching clients I have worked with over the years, who showed up willing to sit in vulnerability and helped me to learn through the process of attempting to help them. You know who you are.

BIBLIOGRAPHY

Carpenter, Harry. *The Genie Within: Your Subconscious Mind—How It Works and How to Use It.* Scotts Valley, California: CreateSpace Independent Publishing Platform, 2003.

Gallup. *Gallup State of the Global Workplace.* New York: Gallup Press, 2017.

Gershon, Michael. *The Second Brain: The Scientific Basis of Gut Instinct and a Groundbreaking New Understanding of Nervous Disorders of the Stomach and Intestines.* New York: HarperCollins, 1998.

Lipton, Bruce. *The Biology of Belief: Unleashing the Power of Consciousness, Matter and Miracles.* Carlsbad, California: Hay House, 2005.

CPSIA information can be obtained
at www.ICGtesting.com
Printed in the USA
BVHW080342260321
603216BV00001B/2

9 781982 262655